WALK EASY WITH ME THROUGH LIFE

By Tim Connor

OTHER BOOKS BY TIM CONNOR

When The Student Is Ready The Teacher Appears
Volume One

When The Student Is Ready The Teacher Appears
Volume Two

Personal Growth Manual

The Voyage

The Soft Sell

WALK EASY WITH ME THROUGH LIFE

By Tim Connor

Library of Congress Catalogue No.: In Publication

ISBN: 0-9606296-1-0

Published by:

Training Assoc. Int'l Inc.
Box 1425
Ann Arbor, MI 48106

313-930-0880

Cover Design: Bryan P. Grose

Illustrations: Bryan P. Grose

Manufactured in United States of America

First Printing: January 1992

We must pass
through solitude and
difficulty, isolation and silence
to find that enchanted place where
we can dance our clumsy dance and sing our
sorrowful song. But in that dance, and in
that song, the most ancient rites of our
conscience fulfill themselves
in the awareness of
being human.

Pablo Neruda, Toward the Splendid City

DEDICATION

To everyone who has ever walked easy with me through life.

Your presence is woven like a tapestry in every word on every page.

I am forever grateful for your joining me on the path through eternity.

Walking at my side for an hour or for years, each of you are a part of me and my journey to enlightenment and discovery.

I pray that your lives have been blessed as you have blessed me with your sharing.

INTRODUCTION

What does it mean to walk easy through life.

Over the years I have been blessed by many people who have walked with me. Each of them contributed to the development of my beliefs, attitudes, philosophy, success and all the lessons I have been learning.

There were lessons in love, anger and happiness. Lessons in grief, pain, patience and joy.

They helped me learn to laugh and cry and most of all how to be real.

Some of them taught me fear and resentment while others how to get over doubts and discouragement.

A few taught me how to forgive and fewer still how to love and how to share my gifts.

They all tried to teach me integrity in my communication and how to deal with life.

Whoever they were, each of them in their own special way gave me the gift of their understanding.

This is a book about the real issues of life, profound feelings and deep desires as well as agonizing pain and struggle.

In these pages I have laid my soul bare to you. These poems are not about fictional characters and events but about real pain and real people. Honest dreams and deep feelings, both internal and external.

This book was written at a time in my life when I was searching deep in my being for answers to the many questions of life. It was a time of great emotional turmoil and profound insight and growth. I was not in a midlife crisis but a period of tremendous introspection and contemplation.

I originally wrote some of these poems to express my deepest feelings and to speed the healing of many years of suppressed frustration, limiting beliefs and grief for a life that could have been so much more. Putting my thoughts on paper was a personal journey and I never expected to publish these self disclosing thoughts and issues. When I wrote the first poem I had no idea that over 150 would follow in less than four weeks. As the number reached 50 I decided to put some of them in my new book at the time "When The Student is Ready The Teacher Appears". When the number reached 100 I decided that these poems deserved a book of their own — the one you are now reading. I am not a poet. But a fellow traveler, like you just trying to walk easy through life. If any of these poems touch you in any way, I will feel blessed.

This is a book about my need to understand myself and life. If some of my thoughts help you to reach new understanding then I share your hope for a better way of life as you walk through life.

This is not a book about philosophy or a treatise on how you should live or feel. It is the outstretched hand of a fellow traveler and a person who has had to face the same questions, feel the same fears, overcome the same doubts and find the same courage to walk easy through life.

Join me now, won't you and let's walk easy through life together.

Tim Connor
Ann Arbor, MI

1991

WALK EASY WITH ME THROUGH LIFE

Walk with me easy through life. Help me celebrate my
victories and be there to catch my tears.
Comfort me in times of grief and help me through the struggle that
life brings.
Life is such a wonderful gift, a miracle indeed. Sharing it with
you adds color to my world and music to my soul.
You can cushion my falls and ease my confusion if we can
walk easy together.
Its memories are like echos from a distant canyon of long ago,
reminding me that my time here is as fragile as the first
rose of summer.

Life brings its strife and joy, passion and
pain, but all of these are like empty vessels without our gentle
union.
I need your counsel and your caring and I will give the same.

I will walk with you if you will walk easy with me though life.

Tim Connor

TO GINA

She glides across the floor like an angel caressing the lives
that come to her, with her smile and her charm.

As I watch her, she is so focused, gently and patiently
guiding her students through a new routine.
Her smile
so engaging and her laugh so captivating as she watches
lovingly the progress made by her willing protege.
I sit, watching her move with such grace and spirit, awaiting
my time with her.

The clock moves snail like.
The minutes seem like hours.
Finally I get a nod and a smile. It's time to begin.
This is a special time for me. Learning from her builds my
confidence and my skill. She is such a delight and a highlight of
my week.
Her soft brown eyes and easy voice urge me on. To stretch
my mind and my uncooperative feet.

She makes the learning fun and playful even when my confidence
leaves me for some other world.

The minutes fly by. I want this time to last. But she has another
life, one I know nothing of.
Our relationship is quite professional,
because she is a pro. Good at what she does and yet she enjoys
every student and every laugh.

I have her for an hour each a week. She guides my growth
so that one day I too will glide the floor with a easiness that will be
a testimony to her talent. I wish these weeks would last forever.
See you next week, Gina.

Tim Connor

WILL YOU JOIN ME ON MY JOURNEY

The room was filled with voices sharing their wisdom and their wit. Each restless soul yearning to be heard, loved and gently caressed by a supportive and patient universe.

I was unaware of how my life was about to change like the flash of summer thunder.

Suddenly,
you filled my vision and sent my spirit soaring.
I was captured by your beauty and the sound of your voice was
like soft music playing
in my mind.
I wanted to shut out an intruding world as it invaded the
intimacy of our meeting and the moments that would fly by
as if time was racing
toward some unknown and impersonal destination.
I wanted to memorize your face and etch your essence on the
screen of my being.

Calene, my world both stopped and started when our eyes met.

I wanted to feast on our newness and devour your thoughts knowing
that soon your memory would be all I would have to carry me
through till our next meeting.

I wanted to smell your breath, feel your hair and cradle your
face softly in the palms of my hands and gaze into the future
through your eyes so loving and kind.
You filled my heart
with wonder and challenged my fragile thoughts.

I wanted the night to last forever.
Talking, learning and touching your being with the deepest part
of my desire to know you,
your fears and fantasies, hopes
and dreams, worries and longings.
In an instant, you were
gone. It was as if the universe was teasing me with the gift of
your presence and
the treasure in your soul.
The night ended, but my head was flooded with thoughts of you and
feelings for you and a vision that toyed with my mind
like a rudderless ship searching for a calm harbor to rest in
peace.

The day began like any other day, little did I know that
it held, waiting in the wings, something significant
that would light a fire in my
heart that had been doused with the pain and frustration of
years of unfulfilled desires.

As I look back on our brief time together, I was filled with
happiness that the universe had after all these years sent
me an angel.

We danced, and it was as if we had been together for
eternity. Your smile touched every fiber of my
being and your movements sent sparks
through every cell of my body.

Morning came with both a vision of time with you and fear
that our meeting was only a fantasy,
a cruel trick of a playful universe.
We hugged and I wanted that hug to last a lifetime.
Then you were gone again like a beautiful butterfly, sharing
your life with an adoring world..

But you will never be gone from my mind, or
my vision. For you are now a part of me and all that is
divine.
The wonderful design of this universe brings to each of us the
gift of love.
Our mission is to grab hold, and never let go.

There is a divine order that sets the stage,
but we must play our parts.

We must fulfill our destiny.

We must yield to the guidance that whispers
from deep within our souls,
trust the universe for your highest good.

Calene, you have touched my spirit and emotions
to the very core of my being. I only pray that you will join me

on my journey.

Tim Connor

YOU ARE ALWAYS THERE

I see you in the beauty of God's creations and I feel you in the music
that touches my mind so softly.
I sense your presence ever with me even though you invade my
reality and are distant in my dreams.

I feel your nearness in all I do and see.

Why must I be tormented by your vision, your laugh and your
illusion.

If I could only hold you and feel the beat of your heart while you feel
my love penetrate your being.
If I could only caress your face and smell the sweetness of your
breath.

If I could only walk hand in hand dreaming together of a future
filled with passion, love, tenderness and growth.

You are always there in the sea of faces that parade through
my life.
If I could only join you on your path through eternity.

You are always there in every waking minute of my life
reminding me of my deepest desire for love and understanding.

If I could only touch your hair, feel your lips against mine and
watch you as you sleep.

My life is filled with your vision and my future is complete
with the fantasy of our togetherness.

Tim Connor

THE PATH

The path leads to nowhere and the path leads everywhere.

As we travel, to each of us it soon becomes clear that no path
is right or no path is wrong, but just is.

We are all,
where we are supposed to be, doing what we are supposed to be
doing and with who we are supposed to be with.

There are no mistakes in the universe.

Others at times, may appear to be lost, but judge not by
appearances.

Life is not always what it seems.

Resist the need to guide or persuade your fellow travelers on the
path. Your wisdom is like wind on the plains or snow falling on
fresh snow. It fades into nothingness.

The messages we heed are all from within. All your words and
gentle counsel will be in vain.
The pace of our journey will vary from day to day and lifetime to
lifetime.
So trust the process of your life and worry not about the
mountain but focus on the terraine at hand.

Concern yourself only with your direction and not the endless road
ahead.

Your future can change in a heartbeat and the vision you held
of your ideal life
can be like the fading color of a summer sunset
or the exploding brightness of a wonderous sunrise.

It is not the pace, the direction or the destination that should
fill your consciousness but only that you continue your journey
with confidence and peace
one step at a time.

Tim Connor

LOVE IS A BRIDGE

Love is a bridge that runs from heart to heart, keeping us
close while we are apart.

It spans the distance between us
whether miles or years, minutes or days.

It is always there for us to cross into the waiting arms
of our beloved
when crisis calls or pain enfolds,
when joy captures or adventure beckons.

Love is a bridge that connects our spirits and our desires
in spite of a doubting world.

When we cross this bridge of love to each other we are safe
in the care of our love for each other.

When we cross the bridge away from each other we never lose
the thread of our love.

For love is a bridge,

a bond that, test as it might, life can never separate our
passion and our devotion.

Love is a bridge that when we are angry or afraid, hurt or alone

always brings us back.

For the bridge between our love runs from heart to heart not
mind to mind, from soul to soul, not day to day, and from

hand to hand.

Tim Connor

LETTING GO

Life to be lived with a peaceful heart requires us from time to
time to let go.

To let go of guilt and let go of resentment.

To let go of the struggle and to let go of expectations.
To let go of trying and to let go of demands.

To let go of rules and to let go of people. To let go of pain and
to let go of ego.

To let go of children and to let go of fantasy. And yes sometimes to
even let go of dreams.

To let go of love that has died and habits that no longer serve.

To let go of stress and to let go of work. To let go of worry
and to let go of friends.

To let go of the old and sometimes let go of the new.
To let go of pride and to let go of toys.

To let go of money and to let go of power, prestige and fame.

To let go of the need to know and to let go of resistance.

But most of all, to let go of self and its urges and its need to be
right.

Tim Connor

TODAY I FELL IN LOVE

I saw her sitting there so curious and so poised, she was my dream
of days gone by.
Her face so fragile, her smile so warm. Her hair glowed like
sunshine kissing the earth.
She was so radiant. How could I not fall in love with her.
How can I tell her, does she
know, can she feel my desire or will it die in me once again.

Was it the image she recalled in me that has been lost in my
memory or is it
a dream of a future that she will fulfill.
She may never know,
how she touched my heart. But her image will be with me always.
Her eyes, her lips so moist and inviting, her walk
so confident and seductive.
Her laugh so young and responsive.
For just a minute in time, I was
18 again or was
it 28.

Who cares. I wanted her to be the one who would cherish and love me.
But the years have taught me better. It is only a distant hope
of love that's past.
I wish I didn't know better.

Tim Connor

Free will does not mean that
you establish the curriculum; only that
you can elect what you want to
take at a given time.

A Course in Miracles

ON THE ROAD AGAIN

The empty faces pass me hurrying to nowhere.
The throngs of people
stack up at the gate waiting for the call, to board their plane
that will hurl them like a bullet to their next stop in life.
I am one of the throng.
As I board, I ask myself, why am I leaving again.
To earn a living,
to gratify my ego, to search for that uncertain future that
stretches beyond the horizon.
We climb, and I listen for strange unfamiliar sounds while
I wonder,
what the person next to me is thinking. Will I make a friend
of this stranger as we share some space in time together,
or will we hold back our need to reach out.
Another safe trip,
and I think, will all my future trips be safe.
But no matter how many times I fly, I will always hate
putting my life in the hands of so many people I do not know.
The taxi hurries,
like a high speed train weaving through the tons of steel
all gliding in the same direction, going nowhere.
If you asked the travelers, they all have a destination in mind
and like me they must
arrive.

But the truth is that we are all passengers traveling through
space and time together moving towards eternity and
a future that is love.
All hotels are the same, the rooms reek of the conformity of life.
This impersonal square will be my home these few days.
While I search the
crowded spaces of this new abode, for adventure, peace, and a friendly
face,
I discover that wherever I go I am alone with my thoughts.
My work is done and now I am heading home. The process

repeats in reverse.
I reflect on the trip, Time has passed, I have given to
life and life has blessed me with the hope that my trip served
some noble purpose. But I am not convinced.
Could I have just stayed home this one time, and hugged my
children, loved my wife and shared with my friends.

Well, I convince myself that the trip was necessary, that the
search for wealth,
fame, success and power is what life is all about.
I'm home now,
and my daughter's smile and open arms make me question the
sanity of my reasoning.
I vow that I will re-think my life's purpose
The phone rings,
I commit, and I am on the road again.
Is this what life is destined to be, strange hotels,
meals alone, and days away from the love I need, from the
people that matter.
I can never recapture, those lost hours, I can
never regain the lost memories of times I
missed. The next time the phone rings,
Tell them I'm out of town.

Tim Connor

LOOKING BACK

I fight the pain of looking back on what could have been,
IF,
Such a powerful word, If I could go back with the knowledge
of today.
But I am here now and those times have made me who I am.
But the unknowns
of tomorrow's possibilities still haunt me.
I missed so much and I miss it still and yet the yearning
to recapture those lost dreams has
lost its sting.
The tears of regret,
still stain my heart. Will these feelings ever leave me or are
they destined to be with me
always.
I can only look back now, no going back, no opportunity to redo
the errors of the past. And
are they errors or is it life as it was meant to be.
Answers, I have a few and questions
so many.
I can only look back with love and understanding and I
can only look ahead with patience and hope.
Tomorrow I will look back on today. My prayer is that
tomorrow's looking back will be done with
a smile.

Tim Connor

CALENE, YOU REMIND ME

Calene, you remind me
of a warm summer day spreading kindness, warmth
and compassion.
You remind me of a gentle ocean breeze, sharing your love,
wisdom and insight with an admiring world.

And, you remind me
of soft beaches, swaying palms and melodies
that soothe the souls of life's weary travelers.

But most of all, you remind me of the faded dreams and
suppressed hopes of my youth that had almost lost their
desire to be set free from the prison of their own making.

And finally,

you remind me that I can trust the design of this
universe with its master plan
for my highest good.

Tim Connor

YOUR SMILE

Your lips part and your smile sends my hopes down
a never-ending path of bliss.

Your perfect lips invite my deepest cravings to hold you
tight while our mouths touch gently yet passionately.

Your smile touches every fiber of my being that longs for love.
Love that lasts and love that brings us together in a union
that transcends time.

Your soft short blond hair is a perfect frame for that youthful
yet understanding smile.

I love your smile, it puts a glow in my heart and wipes away
all the fear and doubt that I am loved.
It keeps my hope alive
that one day we will share life together side by side until
our days are gone.

I've never wanted anyone in my life like the desire I have for
you.

I want to greet each new morning with that smile in my eyes.

I want to drift into sleep each night with my last memory of the
day, your smile and all that it shares.

And when my life is over I want your smile to be my final vision

I take with me from this world into the next.

Tim Connor

DON'T LET THE YEARS KEEP US APART

The years may separate us but we were drawn together to fulfill the
design of a hopeful universe and its mission.

When we are together
I am lost in your essence without regard for the reality
that too many years may keep us from discovering
a union that could bind us to eternity.

Our togetherness and youthful spirits can stand as a witness
to everlasting love and devotion.

Can we,

Will we,
let ourselves put the years that are a shadow to our
newness, out of mind and out of sight,
or will we,
miss the chance for real and lasting love because of our

fear or our ego.

As I look at you, I have never been so sure.

Life brought us together to parade our love before a
cynical world.

Something deep inside me screams, that we are right for each other.

I can only hope that
you at least hear a whisper.

Don't let the years keep us apart from the joy, passion and
love that life has offered to us.

You are a fragile gift of life
to me, one that I will hold in the palm of my hand with

care, understanding

and unmatched devotion.

I will treasure you always if you won't let the years keep us
apart.

Tim Connor

I FELT RESTLESS

The nights stir like a whirlpool of thought.
The days move with an uneasy flow splashing against my consciousness leaving a frothy awareness that my life is about to change.

Where does the restlessness reside inside my being.

Is it some past event, or a future dream, a present hope or a lingering desire.

I wake in the middle of the night, my mind void of reason or care.
I am not tired but full of energy that needs to be harnessed to some worthy end.

Thoughts of you fill my mind and yet I doubt that your unawareness of me is the cause of these sleepless nightts.

There seems to be no rhyme or reason to my alertness or cause for this restless state.

Four hours of sleep is not enough for the day that looms ahead.

A full day of meetings and errands, decisions and adventure.

As well as new learning to speed me toward my understanding of life and reason, purpose and destiny.

This restless feeling that turns nights into days keeps me aware that something is stirring, shaking my being and altering the balance of my life.

But the answers are like a distant mirage. The closer I get the further away is my clarity.

Thoughts of you flood my senses with hope and desire. To have my life settled and at peace knowing that you will be there in all my future days.

But your caution and fear temper my fragile dream of happiness
with you for eternity.

Can it be that this is the birth of a new and lasting love.
And that these restless times are the labor of new feelings
and emotions that demand to be set free from the prison
of their years and the disappointments of the past.

It's 4 a.m. as I write this poem. The words come but sleep flees
like a child chasing a rainbow in the distance.

There is no joy in this endless chain of restless hours.

Unless of course you are restless too, sharing my hope of our
togetherness. And if you are, please tell me so that
the burden of this haunting unknown can leave me to stalk some
other restless soul.

Tim Connor

I LOVE YOU

The words flow with an easiness that is music for my soul.

I love you.

Simple words, yet so powerful when filled with the emotion

of the ages and the devotion of eternity.

I love you.

Not casual words to be spoken to manipulate your feelings
or my lack of self love.

But words to share my deepest
feelings of respect, wonder, support and understanding.

The poets, song writers and lovers through time have
echoed my sentiments. I am no match for their delight and

words so perfect.

But I stand as a monument
to a commitment that I will cherish you always.

I worship the air that you breathe and the beat of your heart.

You are the beginning and the ending,

The forever of my life.

Tim Connor

SUCCESS

Everyone wants success and yet they often don't know when
they have it.

For most, it is the maddening chase toward a better way of life or more
of something. More fame, power, recognition, money or
stuff.
For some it is the understanding of a loving partner, the love
of their child or the people that they can count on when life
throws them a curve.
I am coming to believe that success
is not more. But peace, happiness, contentment and love.

Most of all love.

Real success is not to be sought after in the outer world but
discovered in your inner world. I am not condemning the stuff
of life. We all want the things that life offers. But we don't
need as much as we think we do.
Sooner or later you will discover as well, that real success is to be
found in loving relationships. With your family, friends, strangers
and anyone who crosses your path. It is a kindness
shared, support given and received, listening, giving and caring.
These will endure, while your car rusts, your toys break

and you tire of the temporary gratifications that bring you
what you think is real.
What matters is people.
What lasts is love. What counts are true friends and if you
treasure these you can count yourself a success. If you
lack these but abound in riches and their prize
you will find an emptiness
that will never fulfill your needs or satisfy your desires.

Tim Connor

REAL LOVE GROWS SLOWLY

We meet and then we touch and after a short time
I feel this urge to say I love you.

Can real love come this quickly. My heart says yes but my mind
knows better.
My heart blocks the quiet urgings from my mind. Do I need love
so much that I can convince myself that this infatuation and
emotional pull is real.

I've been infatuated more often that I can remember and my
emotions play tricks on my destiny, but

real love, enduring love, unconditioned love must grow slowly.

The giant oak stands in witness to patience and persistence.
The forsythia blooms quickly, shares its beauty and then fades
into the summer sun and our view, but

real love, supportive love and nurturing love must grow slowly.

The body is willing, the heart follows and we become disillusioned
before the sun sets on another day, but

real love, abiding love, caring love and unselfish love must grow
slowly.

Your beauty and your spirit, your smile and your laugh, your mind
and your joy captivate my being and send my feelings soaring,
but,

real love, spiritual love, life long love must grow slowly.

I want a real love, one that soothes my soul and gives comfort
to my being. I must learn, that real love grows slowly.

Tim Connor

LIFE'S ASSIGNMENTS

Life's assignments are often subtle. They are often hidden in
our desires and camouflaged by our egos' need to satisfy its goal
to control.

Lately I have been struggling with a want I thought was a need,
a fantasy that I knew would never be fulfilled.
Yet I pursued the insanity
of the self destruction of my spirit hoping to rechart the universe
and its design.
While searching for ways to claim my desire I was suddenly
struck like the crack of summer thunder.
This desire for the impossible was
one of life's lessons, one I was hesitant to observe and reluctant
to learn.
To let go of that which cannot be and enjoy what is.

My ego blocks the learning.
My mind will miss the fantasy.
My heart hangs on with a thread of unrealistic hope.
And my spirit knows you came to teach me.
A lesson that was now time to learn.

I will miss the daily thoughts of you that filled my awareness to
overflowing.
But if I am to grow and get on with higher lessons, I must
handle this assignment with easy grace and non-resistance.

I am learning that one of the hardest lessons of life is
letting go.
You came into my life to teach me.
I came into your life to learn.
I hope that in our togetherness I was also a teacher for you.

The mystery of life is that both of us may never know the lessons
we bring to each other and the growth that we stimulate
as fellow students on our journey through life to our
higher selves.

Tim Connor

WHAT WILL IT TAKE

In my fantasy, you are mine but in reality you are a prize
I will never win.

You belong to someone else.
My mind and heart plot together to find favor in your arms.

But when I reach for you, you disappear into the arms of another.

A part of me believes that we will be together despite the will
of an unyielding universe that pleads with me to let go of the
hope that can never be.

I will not rest. I will do whatever it takes to win your heart and
spend my life with you laughing at our youth and sneering at
the plan of life that has kept us apart.

What will it take to beat the odds of life this one time.

Whatever it takes, I will do, for you are the only prize in life
worth living for.

Tim Connor

MY DAUGHTER

I'll never forget meeting the doctor in the elevator. It's a girl.
As he said the words I felt such joy. I knew deep in my heart,
that this would be my only natural child. And I wanted a daughter.
Thank God for this perfect child.

In the early years she was such a joy; funny, happy, and beautiful.
Our family dinners were like a broadway show. She
would entertain us all for hours. Those were wonderful
years. I will treasure them always.

As she grew, her personality became even more playful as she
continued to burn her way deep into the fabric of my heart. I
loved her so very much.
Watching her become a young lady was such a special treat for me.

Then suddenly, divorce ripped her from my life. I was crushed
and my heart was smashed. All my dreams with her were shattered.

I would no longer
watch her move gracefully into womanhood.
I have missed so many little things as well as some of the
bigger events of her life. She will never know the depth of my pain
of this time, lost forever.

We grew more distant. I don't know why.
I missed her so much.
For years watching a movie or a TV show with a father and a
daughter would well the tears up in my eyes.
I felt so cheated and
alone. Why did this happen to us. To lose her this way, was
a cruel trick of life.
Who was to blame. It doesn't matter anymore. I just want my
little girl back. I know I can't regain those lost years and
those unknown memories, but we can begin again to build new
memories.

Now she is back. It has been so long. But it is never too late
to begin anew. We are like cautious absent lovers, carefully
yet purposefully beginning again. I am so grateful. I have another
chance to get it right this time. This time there will be no ego
or pride, fear or immaturity that will hinder our journey back
together.
I love you Heidi.

Tim Connor

WHEN WILL I LEARN

From the depths of my soul I long for your love.

When will I learn that I must,

Get in touch with my real desires and my shallow feelings
that crave for someone to love me.

With every beat of my heart I yearn for you by my side.

When will I learn that all,

the pushing and hoping are like formless shadows
escaping in the night.

With every thought I imagine you in my arms.

When will I learn that,
my beloved will appear when I am ready.

With every step I take I plot in vain for you to want me.

When will I learn that,

when you are ready you will parade into my life
with joy and love, like fireworks filling the sky with

color and passion.
With every breath I take, I want you to feel for me
what I feel for you.

When will I learn that,

your love and our life are in your hands, not mine.

Tim Connor

IT'S MORNING

A new day, a new chance to begin again.
Leaving the cares and mistakes of yesterday behind,
the world quietly affirms you can begin again.
There is hope that the world will be kind today as I move
through the
hours and challenges of
my life.
The bridge between yesterday
and today is the thread of my dreams, my fears and my hopes
together in a pattern that screams you can begin anew.
This day is yours. But deep inside I wonder will today be a
ghost of
yesterday.
But I also know that today is my chance to change tomorrow.
It is morning, I am alive.
Thank you God for this morning.

Tim Connor

THE SEASONS OF LIFE

Life like the seasons has its winter and its springtime, and there
is summer and fall as well.
There are seasons in relationships and seasons in your careers.
The patterns of our lives are as routine as the certainty
of the passing from one season to the next.
Something dies,
and something is born, someone leaves and someone new
comes in.
New opportunities are replaced with struggle and
the struggle gives way to peace.
My impatience for the
passing of the seasons is a sure sign of my lack of trust.

Some people try to hold on to the summertime of their lives,
but summer is always followed by fall. And then sure
enough the winter comes.
Some people try to hold on to a
relationship that has died. By holding on, you slow the coming
of spring.
The universe is in charge of your affairs,
so learn to let go of the details and the seasons when
they have served their purpose.
Be sure and live
each season to the fullest. Such is life. Learn how to live and learn
how to let go.
The seasons were before you were.
And they will be after you are gone. You can't beat the universe.
So flow, relax and enjoy the trip.
Everything will pass. This will pass. Everything that lives must
one day die. This is the law of the universe.
The seasons will come and the seasons will go,
with you or without you.

Tim Connor

IN THE COCOON

Time moves so slowly. I am in the neutral zone of my life.
There are endings and there are new beginnings but between
these are times of reflection and growth.

My weeks are filled with uncertainty and unknowing.

I often feel the frustration of wanting to act but my lack of forward
movement prays on my every waking thought.

I should be busy, but my heart says, peace be still. Your rush
to nowhere is in vain.

There is conflict within me. To do or to be, to move or to flow,
to choose or to listen to that inner voice that whispers within
me.

There are bills to pay and obligations to meet. How long
must I stay in this limbo state nurturing my soul and my spirit.

My body is busy but my mind is a poor servant.
The pressures mount while the doubts persist.
Yet I feel this sense of calm
that all is well and as it should be.

I will one day soon emerge from this quiet time of reflection
better able to live a life
that is truly free. And when that time comes, I know I will
be glad, I trusted my
inner voice that calms my ego mind, be calm, relax.

Honor the wisdom of the universe. It has everything under control.

There will be time for work and time for play, time for love and
time to share.

Tim Connor

MY DESTINY

In the midst of chaos and struggle I have this strong sense,
that one day my life will stand as a shining example of
victory.

That somewhere, somehow at sometime there is greatness
waiting for me.

Now, the question is how would I define greatness. Maybe I'm
there and just don't know it.
My ego says that there must be more. More of something or
more of everything. That my greatness is a future event yet
to be, or an accomplishment waiting to be realized.
But as I survey my life,
at what is its midpoint, I must admit I have done more, seen more,
tried more and failed more than most.

If I was to die before this poem were finished I would feel cheated.
Are there more poems to write and more books to create.
There is more in me that wants to be set free. There is more love
to express, more wisdom to gain and more ideas to share.
So what is my destiny.
It is to finish this poem and
write another. It is to give love today as well as tomorrow.

It is to learn today and share what I have learned.

It is not some distant prize or award on the horizon of my
life, but living well today.

Tim Connor

CONFLICT

The pain of conflict keeps the words unspoken, words
that if said would end the pain.
As you can see,
I seem to avoid that which can lead to peace. I struggle
with the hurts that I imagine would result from
my honesty.
I have learned my lessons well. But in my heart
I am learning that your anger or your
disapproval is not always for me but for my actions.
But there are those times,
when in years gone by. There was judgement and
criticism in your words.
You expressed, so
I withdrew. To that safety zone where I knew,
you could not reach
to cause me pain. Yet in my deepest self,

I felt the pain of unexpressed fears, feelings, hopes
and dreams.
My hope has been,
that you would help me release the words,
and then the pain of unexpressed conflict
that I carry with me from day to day.

As the days pass,
and I feel secure, we are friends again, on the surface at least.

But because of the memory of the hurt and the habits I've learned,
it is only a matter of hours before I withdraw,
once again into my inner prison. Where all seems safe,
yet freedom is gone.
The pattern repeats, the pain persists.
Some day soon I will decide that it is time for a change,
to no longer hide from the feelings I fear and the words that
tear my confidence to shreds.
The peace I desire can be mine if I will only see that
conflict is real and a part of life, not to be avoided but confronted
with love.

Tim Connor

PLEASE LISTEN TO ME

Won't you please listen to my pain and my joy.
Let me share with you without
your judgement and distraction.

Please hear my grief and open you ears to my needs.
I have a story to tell but it is meant for your mind only.

If you won't hear me then my story will die a slow
agonizing death within me.

Tim Connor

The important thing
is this: To be ready at
any moment to sacrifice
what we are for what
we could become.

Charles Dubois

MY LIFE

How do I define the indefinable, how do I explain the
unexplainable.
It is, it has been and it will be for how long I cannot say.
But I feel blessed to have lived it all.
I've had my share of pain and struggle and I've enjoyed
love and laughter.
There have been people who have cared and some who
didn't,
events that taught me and events that seemed to have
no apparent meaning.
The search for understanding continues in earnest. The
questions abound the answers are few.
The lessons are many while my self love grows.

Where will it end and how, who will I have become when my
time is up. I cannot say. All I can do
is love the time I have regardless of appearance.
There were times, many times when I had wished my life
were different, but I made it what it is, so I must accept
the results for what they are.
The pain I brought and the joy I experienced, they are all mine.
My life has been like a song, a song of hope, a song of
despair,
and a song that has many more verses to sing.
The melody is the same,
but the words are evolving as I move into new insight, wisdom
and new feelings. Unknown territory yes, but I am the
composer of my life and I can use a solitary guitar or an
orchestra to express my oneness with the universe.
Let's all sing.

Tim Connor

AS I LOOK AHEAD

I have been blessed with a good mind, a healthy body and
the opportunity to grow and learn.

As I look ahead down the road to the days and months that
will one day be my present, I look with hope and optimism
that life will continue to bless my journey.

I know there will be new
struggles, more pain and disappointments and yet I feel
a sense of positive anticipation as I begin each new day.

There are new people to meet, ideas to share, love to give
and someone who will come into my life who will
brighten my days and bring peace to my nights.

I can't be certain what lies ahead.
The details are like shadows waiting for the light, but I am
confident that life will give me what I can handle and cheer
my passing.

There is one thing I know as true. Today I create my
tomorrows.
Oh, not the exact picture, but the theme and the outcome.
So it is that I must look ahead with my eyes wide open
while I keep my heart in the present. That's where my life is
lived,
in each single now moment as it passes.

Tim Connor

THE DISTANCE BETWEEN US

It's hard to say when the distance between us began to grow.
Was it a word, a deed not done or an emotion left
unexpressed.
Whenever or wherever it started, the pain of my loneliness
in our relationship stings my heart.

Our eyes no longer meet in love but in despair. Our touch
is a faded memory and our words are like the words of strangers
in the lonely night.

How could this happen. We were so in love. Our hearts and minds
were full of anticipation for the days and years ahead.

Now all we share are the ghosts of long faded feelings and the
common space we call our home. It is not a home but
a prison that pretends to be loving. But it is not loving it
is cold and aloof.

This is love slowly dying. A painful death at that.
Can we, will we, close this emotional distance between us,

Time will tell and yet the clock is working against us,
It will take both of us,
to heal the wounds and ease the pain of these times so near.

I am willing, but in my heart I know your love has died.

So as the days pass, I slowly prepare my heart for its breaking.

Not an easy task as I recall those special times we've
shared as one.

Tim Connor

WHY DO YOU REFUSE TO GROW

I've tried to help you in so many ways. To ease your pain
and speed your growth. And coach you in your frustration.

But you continue to refuse my loving urgings.
Your pain is yours but I feel it as well.
I struggle with you while I know that you, must be the answer to your life.

I have learned that I cannot help you, try as I will.
I can only coax and support you in your views and in your
stubbornness.
But it doesn't stop my desire for your highest good.
You say you know what you want, but you resist the chance to change.

We are all on our own path of discovery, and yet we are all on the same path.
I can't discover for you,
that is a gift from you to you.

I will hold out my hand to you to help you in your search
for peace and contentment. But you must take my hand.

Won't you please join me on the path of
enlightenment.

Tim Connor

LIFE'S JOURNEY

It began so many years ago. So joyous was the occasion, my
coming into the world. It was a special event for all.

My early years were full of growing and learning. Becoming and
trying.
These early years were followed by a time of play and challenge.
The challenge to discover my real self. But I was too young
for this searching. The real search would come much later.

There was not time for questions and little patience for
answers.

I was still becoming. The road ahead was uncertain. But I did
not mind, or even care. I was in my youth. There would be
time to learn life's lessons.

There were lessons then,
that if well learned, could have made my later years less painful
and more secure.

As I pass through mid-life, I see the error of my youthful ways.

So now I must tend to the matters at hand. Living well
in a changing world while my thoughts, feelings and being
are changing as well.
Because before too long, there will be no more years ahead when
I can look back and take what I learned and use it in my
present to change my ways.

There are only a few lessons that must be learned before my time
is up.
How to accept love and share love.
And how to be real.

Tim Connor

BPG
91

RAINBOW'S END

The mist rises slowly from the glassy surface of the inlet
as I prepare for a day of solitude and reflection sailing my
Rainbow's End.

There is so much to do and plans to make to ensure a safe passage.
Sailing is kind of like life in many ways. There are so many
unknowns and some of the best plans are in vain.

I love my time with Rainbow's End. It is therapy
in the midst of a chaotic world. There I am alone with the
wind, sea and sun.

The sound of the water splashes against her bow, it is a welcome
sound, I am making headway to my destination. But it is not
the destination that is my goal, it is the journey.

The wind and sun soothe my mind and soul as I drift back
to days gone by and of days ahead.

I have a dream to sail her around the world some day. To
introduce her to new places and people who will fill our memories
with sights and sounds of exotic times and
new adventures together.
She is my trusted friend. Responsive, forgiving, supportive,
nonjudgmental,
loving and secure. I can take her anywhere. There is nowhere
that I don't feel safe with her.

She and I will share untold new experiences together as we move
through life.

She will not be jealous or envious of the other woman in my life.
She will welcome her lovingly.
Together we will reach new heights of understanding,
appreciation and love. We will live life to the fullest,
searching the deep blue for the kind
winds that will carry us
with joy and exhilaration toward peace and happiness.

As I slowly wake leaving the darkness behind I realize I have

been dreaming once again of Rainbow's End and the pleasure
she will give me.

Or have I been dreaming of the love of my life, that one person
who will help make all my dreams come true.

Some day both dreams will be a part of my life. And I will
share the love, hope and joy of each dream with both
my loves. Together we will cross the oceans of time,
sharing new experiences that will bind us together as
life's partners. Our love will be as strong as the tides,

patient as the sun and as passionate as the wind.

Tim Connor

ALONE

The days move so slowly the nights fade into nothingness.
The dawn comes and it begins
again. One day is like the next. I search for a smile, a kind
word, a friendly face, someone to fill my emptiness and my
thoughts.
My quiet fears blossom,
in my aloneness that these empty days will last too long.
That they may last forever.
There is an endless stream of errands, meals alone, books to read
that become my friends yet they cannot fill the pain of my
solitude.
I wait for the phone to ring, should I go out or not, what time to
bed. So many major decisions. The clock is not my friend.
It is a constant reminder of what my life could be,
but is not.
Another day is gone.
I must overcome this need to keep busy, and learn to love
the quiet.
The emptiness is not in my days and nights but in me.
This time will pass, but when.

Tim Connor

INTIMACY

There are times when we feel so close. Why won't those moments
last.
There are times when I feel so free to be, with you, who
I am afraid to be alone.
This trust, compassion and openness comes so seldom
but it is so beautiful when it does.

What is intimacy. I know how the spiritual teachers
and counselors define it. They may be right but do they
experience it or do they describe it only.

Is it a look, a touch or a feeling or knowing that I am loved,
as I am, and accepted for who I am becoming.

One thing I know, it is opening the deepest parts of me to you for
you to view and inspect. It is bearing my biggest fears,
true feelings and wildest dreams to you for you to ponder.

You can listen or you can act as if you care. You can share or you can
shut me out. You can call me childish and immature and
you can critique my every thought.
But when I find the courage to be real, I hope you will be too.

And in that time wherever we are and whatever we are doing we will
join together as one.
As the years go by I pray that these times will increase as our
oneness unfolds. In a world of superficial charm and
contempt, we can be an island, a safe haven for love to grow.

And we can teach the world together, there is time to
listen, time to share and time to care.
And that time is now. And that place is here.
And that person is you.

Tim Connor

HOW OLD AM I

In some ways I am a child and in other ways an old man.
I'm 26, 18, 39, 50 and 75 and others depending
on my mood or yours.
Why is age so important.
Why is it a barrier to much that would bring joy and peace.
I know I am younger than my years but do you.
Or are you hung up on a few grey hairs or a few extra pounds.
What is youth and middle age. When am I young and when am
I old.
I have the hopes of a 6 year old, the mind of a 60 year old, the
body of a 40 year old and the spirit of a teenager.
So how old am I. I am both younger and older than you.
So relax, lighten up and enjoy who I happen to be at
any given moment. I am here now
that is all that matters.

Tim Connor

FAITH

Often my faith is tested more than I care to admit. My lack
of patience is a witness to my shallow trust.
I know that life always gives me what I need even though
my wants may go unsatisfied.
There are times
when I confuse my desires with my needs and believe I know
what is best for me.

My arrogance says I want it now. My humility says God is in
charge, relax.
My fears question God's calendar, my hope says be calm.

My humanness judges by appearances while my divinity sees
beyond what is real to what is possible.

My life is not a test to pass or fail. It is a human expression
of divine love and will.

So why do I worry about all the human issues that confront me
daily. Why do I often question my desires.
Because I am not yet a perfect example of faith expressed.

Faith is the substance of things hoped for, the evidence of things
not seen.

If I could see it, feel it, own it or have it I wouldn't need any faith.

There are only two choices. To have faith in divine love, abundance
and good for my life or not to have faith.

Living with faith is better than living without it.

Tim Connor

WHERE HAVE THE YEARS GONE

It seems like just yesterday that the days of my youth were
ever with me.

There were no worries to speak of and my future loomed
ahead with a carefree recklessness, that would soon be replaced
with the responsibility of fatherhood.

I moved swiftly through my days more concerned with who would be
Friday's date than where next month's mortgage payment
was. Those were stress-free easy days.

Oh the wonder of youth, where did I leave you, was it in
my marriage or my search for success.
I would not go back, now,
to those days but I would like to recapture the feelings
of freedom and spontaneity that governed
that time of my life.
The time has passed so quickly. My daughter was born
then in an instant she was a woman. My flat top was the rage
now my hair spray is a constant companion.
I could run for days on a few hours sleep, now I need days of
rest to play for a few hours.
I was stronger then but I am wiser
now. Why must one replace the other.
The days now are good, but if I could have one wish, it
would be to ease the pace of their passing.

I never thought I would be this old, and yet I feel so young.

Like it or not, accept it or not, the years speed by.
I want to put so much into these days but I am often at a loss
for what. Time can be our friend or our enemy.

In my youth there was time for everything. Each choice now is a
decision to ponder.
Today there is less time in front of me than has passed.
But there is still time to be young, if not in years then in spirit.
I did not leave my youth behind. It is with me now waiting
to be set free.

Tim Connor

WHY WAS I THE LAST TO KNOW

Your friends knew.
    The children knew.

Your hair dresser knew.

Your employees knew.

I really knew, but I didn't want to know.

Tim Connor

DIVORCE

The last thing on people's minds when they marry is that
one day they will find themselves alone again.
Thoughts of love, passion, hope, caring and trust fill the
minds of two lovers who
have come together, drawn together by the bonds of life.

Where does it happen, how does it happen that these
two lovers and friends soon drift apart in agony.

The love fades, the support flees and the sex is a burden,
if there is any sex at all.

Something has died. Or was it ever really alive.

Can two people so much in love, love so little, so soon.
It happens all too often and well before their love has had
any chance to grow.

When it does, no one wins. I wonder who loses the most.

Who suffers the most. Who feels the most grief and who
ends up lost in life.
I've been lost and I know the pain and I've felt the sting of
lasting grief,
that seemed to have no end.
It never really leaves, it is just hidden from view.

Someone new helps us forget and bury the pain of loss
deep into our being. It is always there though, ready to surface,
with a timely cue from the world of reality.

The mind works overtime, for days and nights
it re-lives the before and it fears the unknowns of tomorrow.

The heart bounces back and forth from anger and resentment,
to frustration and fear. There are few positive thoughts
here.

The time will come for growth and learning, but for now
there are only tears and anguish.
Who do I blame. It can't be me and there is only you, so you
become the focus of my anguish.

Why did you do this to me, my life is in shambles, my emotions
live on the ragged edge of disaster.
Can I really blame you, or is it life that is at fault, or people,
fantasies and expectations
unrealized.

Will this time ever pass. If you ask me now I would say no.
I have been through this before and it's still the same,
nothing better and no worse, it just seems so.

It doesn't really matter why it happened. It just did. But I long
for relief from these feelings and hopelessness.

Much time has passed now and yet the thoughts of you remain.
The only difference between then and now is that I know

you have left me behind in both thought and emotion and you

have begun your new life as if the old life never was.

Oh yes you are still there in my thoughts, but I am getting
better. I am healing at last. I can feel the gradual return
to who I am and the glory and joy of life.
Your emotional distance speeds my cure.

I have so many questions but I know there will be no answers.

I must live forever without the answers. I will do it, I can do it.

I must do it.

Tim Connor

MY WOUNDED CHILD

Years ago the child in me was wounded by the world, well meaning
as it was.

The scars of yesterday remain etched on by being, taking their toll
on all my days and nights,

Looking back I can see the errors of those around me. Little did
they know the pain and suffering they would bring me.
Now that I am older I search for that loving open child that was.

But he remains in hiding from the pain that today might bring.
I want to set him free,
so that my life can be anew. But to reach him I must look
deep into the pain and the past. He protects himself with
games that he plays. Games of guilt and anger and fear and
resentment.
There is no winner in these games. For me to be free he must be
free to act and react not as the world expects
but as he feels is right.
Those around may not understand the turmoil and grief I feel for
his suffering. I'm not even sure who he is anymore but I know
when he comes forth that I will love him.
For he is the me I used to be and want to be again.
The me that is real.
I have missed him all these years and it is time for him to have
his say. To guide my feelings and my growth. It is time for him
to set my world right. He has been gone too long.
I welcome him now to brighten my future and change my ways.

To help me laugh and love again in ways only he knows how.
For when he returns, you may not know me. But that's ok,
for he will love you just the same. He will bring a smile to your
face and love to your heart.

Tim Connor

TODAY

Enjoy this day
And be of good cheer
Every day is a Gift from God
TODAY
I will use this day
To Know – And to grow
To Love – And to give
To Share – And to care
TODAY
I will listen to my world
Its joy and its pain
Its laughter and its tears
TODAY
I will be part of life
Not an onlooker
I will get involved
With this day –
and
Leave a little of me behind
In someone, something or somewhere
TODAY
I matter – You matter – We all matter

Tim Connor

True teachers
use themselves as
bridges over which they invite
their students to cross; then, having
facilitated their crossing, joyfully
collapse, encouraging them
to create bridges
of their own.

Nikos Kazantzakis

TRUTH

What is truth. Sometimes I think I know, then as soon
as I find the answers are clear, truth betrays me again.

Was it truth that betrayed me or was it that I never really
knew truth to begin with.

Life is about truth, not my truth but yours and your
willingness to have your concept of truth
challenged.

To talk of truth is to assume a certain arrogance or pride
of some special insight or wisdom that the universe
has bestowed on you and me. Life has a loving way of
humbling us at just the
right time in just the right way,

Most of life is paradox. The secret to living freely and with
peace,
is to interpret what you think is truth accurately, and to test
it against the constants of the universe.

Then to live the best way you know
how, with that you've got at the time.
No easy task,
given the billions of variables from one second to the next.

The best we can hope for, is peace without knowing,
love with uncertainty and wisdom without evidence.

And faith in the midst of questions and controversy.

Sorry, no consolation
here. I'm searching for the same truths you are.

Tim Connor

MY SOUL MATE

Is there such a thing as a true soul mate, that one person who,
without effort,
or wishing is that single life that can add to the quality
of our existence with a natural flow that can stand
the test of time.
Someone who feels what we feel, believes in what we believe
in and loves what we love.

Do we really find, or do we create or compromise,
to have that one and only person that the universe quietly
whispers,
this is the one for you, you were born to be together.

My mind has lied to me so many times before. That you were
the one, my true soul mate. Then you were gone. Can I ever
trust my mind again.

Is there really such a thing as a kindered spirit or is it my ego,
that manipulates
your being into that mirror image of my mind's fantasy.

My heart and mind so often seem to cooperate in the
scheme to convince me that it is possible that there is one true
soul mate for me.

If so, what are the chances, in this life, of ever finding that
solitary life that is my destiny. Unlikely. Yet the
universe plots for my good. Do I wait and trust or do I search
and hope.

I like searching and hoping. I feel in control. Yet my searching
and hoping has been in vain. You still elude my grasp.
Is there an answer. I've been wrong more than I have been right.

I'd rather be happy than right. But my ego likes the idea
of a soul mate. I need to kill my ego. My heart says to trust,
my mind says search.
I think I will listen to my heart this time.

Tim Connor

DECISIONS, DECISIONS

So many choices so few real options. I can only do one thing
at a time and there is only one place I can be.
I am limited to being with one person so I must choose.
Every decision eliminates all other choices.
Yet I want the power to have it all. What if I make the wrong
choice and is there even the possibility of wrong choices.

Once I commit, am I doomed
to make that decision the right one.
So many right choices have turned out wrong and many wrong
choices have gone well. Is there some secret to deciding well,
or is it just an arbitrary turn of the wheel. Should I plan,
evaluate and decide or let life, with its understanding,
show me the way, taking what comes. I am not a tree or a dog.
I can think and anticipate the consequences of my choices. But
to what avail. My whole life can change in an instant.
A person arrives, a person leaves, opportunity presents itself,
and a business fails. Who can know what is coming next.
Is my choosing like whistling in the wind.
The power of choice
was given to me. A gift from God to use with love. Love of self,
love of others and love of life.
I have spent hours of my life trying to be clever and outwit destiny,
invariably to look back with a smile and see that all the hours
could have been better spent.
The path of life is full of forks in the road.
And whichever fork I take, there will
be another fork, and another and another until the final fork.

In my arrogance I am in charge of my life and it's decisions.
But in my humility I am used by God for His higher good.
He gently guides me toward a destiny of his choosing.
The steps along the way are mine to take, but they ultimately
lead to his higher purpose for my life.

So it becomes clear, to choose well, I must only listen to that inner
voice. And then find the courage, faith and patience to surrender
to that inner inspiration that is so strong.
The road ahead will never be clear or certain. As I act, I must
learn to trust my choices and the source of the guidance within me.

Tim Connor

WHY CAN'T YOU HEAR WHAT I CANNOT SAY

So many times I have spoken to you without words, but you did not
hear.
How could you, you only saw what you wanted. My unspoken
feelings could never replace the need for words to share my
fears, hopes, and fantasies. I continued to try but you
still couldn't sense the meaning behind my expression
and the frustration in my mind.

I'll never know why I didn't have the courage to just say
what I felt, thought or believed. Was it pride
or weakness that kept the words back.

Sooner or later the words must be spoken out loud. And the
longer it takes the more stress I feel. Why can't you make it
easy for me, and read me as I stand in silent witness
to my inner struggle.

I know the answer to that question. Your role is not to make
my life easy but to help me, make me better.
And until I learn to use the words that are stored up within me,
I will stall this lesson of honesty that yearns to be learned.
So have patience, I am
learning. But there are so many dreams, fears and thoughts that
need expression. With time, love and understanding I will
get there.
But I can't do it alone. I need your subtle encouragement and
awareness that I am trying.
Your compassion
will be rewarded with the knowledge that I love you enough
to trust you with my fragile self. And that no one
else in the world has ever had access to this inner world of mine.
Just you.
And you will love what you see when you get in. Because I, like
you am a loving perfect child of God.

Tim Connor

GOD, WHERE ARE YOU

I know you are here and everywhere but I seem to have so much
trouble finding you.
I've searched the books, and the universe, the churches and
the splendor of nature. I've looked deep inside myself only
to find that there are no answers.
Am I asking the wrong questions, am I not hearing your
words of guidance.
I see evidence of your presence everywhere, the face of a
child,
the changing of the seasons, the beauty of friendship and the
wonder of love. But the frustration persists. I search and I
do not find.
Am I looking in the wrong places or in the wrong way.
Confusion is now my constant companion.
I hear counsel on how to get in touch with you, through
prayer and quiet. But
I hear nothing. I want to know and feel your presence
to know your spirit in
me.
Should I stop the search. I think I will for now.
Just knowing you are there is
enough.

Tim Connor

A STUDENT IN LIFE

There are so many opportunities to learn, to grow and to
understand.
Life sends us a continual flow of teachers to guide and to
challenge
and to help and to correct. There are times,
when I am ready to listen and so many times when I
haven't.

But the lessons are always present. Is it my stubborness
or my ego, or is it my pride that stalls the learning.
If I could only get out of my own way,

I could learn when the time is right, the first time the lessons are
presented.
I could save myself so much pain.
The path of growth and understanding
is forgiving for a time. It is patient and loving for a time.
But time is running out. The pain of unlearned lessons haunts
me. The memories of
previous lessons not learned is etched on my soul.

They are repeated, louder now. But I still refuse to learn.
What will it take to master that
urge to resist. My reluctance to grow has a price. A price
that was low at first. But with each new opportunity to learn
the price went up. And in the future days the price will
be higher still. I could reach the higher ground if I would let the
learning come. There, the rewards are sweeter.
The answer is simple,
be a student able and loving. Love all your teachers
that life sends your way,
for life knows your needs and resist as you will, life says, I'll
be back another day.

Tim Connor

MY FRIEND IS GONE

He was the closest thing I ever had to a real friend.
He listened and cared and loved and shared.
His spirirt was bright and his demeanor calm.
We called him Flash,
but his name was Randy. He touched all of our lives with his
courage and his faith. He loved life and
lived every minute of it. But death took him and too soon
I might add.
The cancer took him from us and he was still a young man.
At his funeral, I cried.
Were the tears for me, the friend I had lost or for him and his loss.
The tears were for both of us.
Your picture is always with me as a reminder of how fragile
life can be and how
quickly if can be over. You are with me everywhere.
Your friendship touched my life.
I am softer, kinder and wiser because you lived and were
my friend.

Tim Connor

YOU ARE MY MIRROR

When I listen to you, am I hearing you or a reflection of me.
When you hear my words is it me you hear or am I your mirror.
We are a reflection of each other in reality, but in fact, it is almost impossible to be an honest witness to these images.

I see my hopes in your eyes,
I feel my dreams in your soul, I sense my frustrations in your words and actions.
In a way I am you and you are me.
Painful as it may be to confess this truth, I know that I must be open to your reflection of me.
You are my teacher, teaching me what life has decided is your special gift to me. The gift of my own reality.
Even though I may resist your teaching, I am grateful for your caring and honesty.
You may not even be aware, that you are teaching me.
But I have learned, that life's classroom, is always in session.
When we talk, share, disagree, love and argue we are teaching each other.
The lessons may be subtle or like the 4th of July, but they are always there if we will look past the images that our egos protect.
To know ourselves is to see openly our true selves in each other.
To have the courage, to look inside and to let go of our resistance to change, is to love ourselves.
The accuracy of my reflections and your love help make my growth possible.
You are the best mirror I have ever had, and I love the opportunity to share this time of growth with you.

Tim Connor

RUSHING TO TOMORROW

Yesterday is gone. Its hurts and its joy. Its success and its mistakes and its frustrations and its desires.

Tomorrow is like a wisp of wind that comes and goes in an instant, teasing me with hope, unfulfilled aspirations and concern for a world I may never know.

Today, that's the miracle. Today is where my tomorrows are born and my yesterday's buried.

And now, this minute, is where life is lived one second at a time.

So why do we ignore each now second as it passes as we rush into the future, leaving behind so many feelings not felt, words not spoken and love withheld.

What is this lure of tomorrow that is life's charade that draws us out of our now moments and into the ghost of our future.

Now is when I hug my child. Now is when I say I love you. And now I smell the aroma of life and nature's gifts.

None of these can be done tomorrow. And yet, if I wait, one day there will be no more tomorrows and I will have missed all my todays.

Tim Connor

AGAINST THE WALL

Have you ever had your back against the wall wondering which
way to turn or whether to turn at all.

Has your world ever been in chaos caving in from every possible
direction.

Have your guts been upside down and your mind twisting like a
tornado destroying everything in its path.

Has your fuse been so short that any spark would send the
explosion of your emotions cascading to the very farthest depths
of this universe.

Has discouragement ever been an unwelcome companion.

My friend, you are not alone.

I've felt the turmoil and the fear, the anxiety and the plaguing doubt.

I'll admit I've felt like giving up and throwing in the towel.
And I've been there more than once, once too often I fear.

I've questioned,
are these times to test and mold me or to break me so that God
can begin again with me to build a mind that is clear and a
spirit unencumbered by pride and ego.

I've never found
an answer to that question, but I know that when I have been
surrounded by the villains who would bury my hope, kill my joy
and subdue my passion that I didn't really care what the answer
was.

My lack of trust has often pushed me near the edge of disaster.

And though I teetered very close to the rim of despair, God always
brought me back.

Stronger, wiser, better.

The road back was slow and required a new outlook on life to reach
a point of safety. There was always light at the end of the
tunnel but to see it required focus, faith and right thinking.
But most importantly it often required that I just turn
toward the light. It was always there but behind me as I
traveled in the wrong direction toward the darkness.

Difficult times build character they say. Trials build strength and
adversity adds to humility.

These are all worthy traits,
but when I am deep in self doubt and fearful about tomorrow.

I must learn to let it flow and then let it go.

Tim Connor

THINKING

Thoughts, useless thoughts, are recycled again and again through

the portholes of my mind. What is the source of all this turmoil
and randomness. As I try to focus my
mind on positive ideas, there you are, and I brought you in
with all the anger and fear, guilt and resentment, blame and
confusion.

I am not the master of my thoughts or my thinking.
These are my thoughts not yours so why must I turn over the
control of my mind to you again and again.

The day's disappointments and life's frustrations wander in and
out of my consciousness with a reckless agony that punishes me
until I can take no more.
So for a brief moment my mind is finally quiet,
Then it begins again,

There is no noble purpose served by this lack of control. My mind
is the servant of all my emotions, all my fears and all my future
plans.
And all this energy could be better spent, enjoying the scenery
and this frozen moment in eternity.
I will never experience this now again, ever. I must learn to
wash my mind clean of this futile behavior.

I must become the master of my mind before I go crazy.

Tim Connor

SOME THINGS NEVER CHANGE

The divorce rates are up and births are down.

Old people still yearn for a receptive ear and children want it all.
Everyone seems like they are getting older while the years
continue to add wrinkles and aches to this body you call home.

Recessions come and go and interest rates still rise and fall.

Winter still follows fall and pain follows pleasure and pleasure
follows pain.

Life is still difficult for many and a disaster for some.

People still hurt the ones they love and spend time with people who
won't be there in their

need. People who are there because of the shallowness
of their own lives.

Everyone is reaching for more while they no longer enjoy
what the years have provided.

And the searchers continue to search the heavens for the answers
to their life when all they need to do is look inside and the
search would end.

Tim Connor

WILL YOU MEET ME HALFWAY

Will you meet me halfway;

on the road back to understanding
as we try to overcome the tension and the silence.

As we recall all that we were in better days gone by.

As we try to capture all those loving feelings that seem so distant now.

As we try once more to cement the bond of our love so fragile and so young.

As we try one more time to heal our pain and disappointment.

I will meet you more than halfway if you will meet me halfway.

Tim Connor

LET IT FLOW THEN LET IT GO

Unexpressed emotions bury themselves deep in the body to
one day surface again.
And they will have their way.

They may surface in a new relationship or they may quietly stalk
you as your years slowly move ahead,
taking their toll on your health or your serenity.

Stuffed grief and pain, anger and
resentment serve no useful ideal. They are enemies to your
peace.

Resentment held in check will play games with your sanity
and you will not win the day.

Anger denied does not affect the other in your life but it will
keep you locked in your own personal hell on earth.

To find peace,
let your emotions flow and then let them go.

Tim Connor

WORKING OUT

Some come to build their bodies as if to temples of some aging
Goddess and their youth. And some come to sport their
curves to an adoring world.
Others come to
talk, bond and network while others survey the sea of bodies
in search of love.
There is a superficial charm in all this sweat.

I go hoping to slow the aging of my body while building the energy
to carry me through the trials of life.

It's harder now than in years past to preserve the look that once
I took for granted.
So now I just try to keep up, knowing that as the years pass
I will need to find joy in the picture of my youth
that is fading with every day.
While I struggle with one more workout,
It is not ego that keeps me going but the fear that this body
will one day desert me in my need.

Tim Connor

THE CARRIBEAN

My favorite paradise is the chain of leeward isles that dot the
Carribean like a pearl necklace in stark contrast to the blue-green
blanket they adorn.
The white puffs of air float
lazily by as the shadows come and go caressing the dense hills
and soft white beaches below.

As our small plane circles for its final approach my cares finally
leave me as I peer out the window like in a dream.

These islands call to me in winter,
but the lure is hidden in the responsibilities of career and life.
They call to me in my dreams but who can live in a dream world
untouched by stress and pressure.

But this is not a dream now. I have seven days to feel the balmy
nights and the soft breezes while the scent of a million
flowers fills the air with an aroma that is heaven sent.

The music collides with my reality, the cool water washes away
my fears and the warm sun slowly soothes my troubles.

Sailing these waters without a care for tomorrow is my
fantasy.

As I sit on the beach, my thoughts are with all the small white
specs that slowly glide past my vision.

My spirit is with them even though I am landlocked once again.

But how much better it is to be
landlocked in this paradise than in my office in Ann Arbor.

Tim Connor

BPG 91

I CANNOT BEGIN AGAIN

Why must I begin again.
The memories of past beginnings haunt me like a fog that
has no beginning and no end.

If I had known I would have to begin again, would I have begun
again with you.

I don't think so.

It's not that the beginnings are so hard. It's leaving the old
endings behind while they plague my consciousness as I try to
move ahead with newness.

Where do I start, when do I start, why must I start again.

Will this new beginning end requiring me to begin again.

All I have to do is take one new beginning at a time, but my mind,
with each new beginning has lost some of its will to try again.

Tim Connor

HAVE YOU EVER

Have you ever felt silly as your eyes followed the love fantasy of
your life only to be discovered in your uncertainty and your lust.

Have you ever gone out of your way to follow, unseen, that ideal
love object only to lose him or her in the crowd.

Have you ever held back, wanting to reach out to break the ice,
but not knowing how or when.

Have you ever wished you could take back those silly words
that tried to impress, when all they did was send your
pride running to hide wherever it was safe.

Have you ever surrendered yourself in your fantasy only to wake
up discouraged and lost.

Have you ever missed the chance to fulfill your hope because
your doubts unraveled at the moment of truth.

There is only one place, here, and only one time, now.

So the next time you find yourself face to face with your
dream, go for it.
You won't get another chance.

Tim Connor

BILLS, BILLS, BILLS

The phone rings and they want a payment. The mail arrives and
it's bills, bills, and more bills.

Why do these people often feel, that the nastier they are, the
more inclined I will be to want to pay them first.

They all seem to take it so personally, like I owe them the
money and not their company.

I'm doing the best I can to satisfy all. I have overstretched myself
again with great dismay. I don't like the stress and the pressure
that is with me always. I know that I brought it upon me but
someday I will learn.
I try to focus on solutions but they keep bringing me back to the
problems.

I had hopes when I bought, that the sale would go through or the
check would arrive.
Unfortunately for you and for me, neither happened so here I sit
wondering what to do and what to say.

It's times like these that I feel like chucking it all and heading south
to some desolate isle, where even the gulls don't know my name
or what I owe.

I think I can make it through one more day. But I'm learning
to hate this phone.

I'm not waiting for my ship to come in just
today's mail.

Tim Connor

IF I LOVED YOU MORE

If I loved you more would you love me too.

And if I loved you more would you try to understand
who I am and love me still.

If I loved you more could we be friends and share hopes and
dreams.

If I loved you more would you listen to my fears and honor my
frustrations.

If I loved you more would you want to share time
together as we share this common space.

And if I loved you more maybe I wouldn't disappoint you so often
with my words and in my deeds.

If I loved you more could I be real and vulnerable once again.

And maybe if I loved you more, I could love you even more.

Tim Connor

THE FIRE INSIDE

I love people who feel a passion for life and their mission to serve with their special gifts.

If there is a fire in your gut there's bound to be a few sparks flying our of your mouth.

So many people live lives of quiet desperation trudging through life with an aimless walk and a backwards glance.

Now don't get me wrong, I loath that fake brand of enthusiasm that wanes with every passing adversity.

Passion and enthusiasm are being not acting or trying.

They come from the inside out not the outside in. It is not a switch that you flick when you need a burst of energy or you are trying to impress.

People who have it, do more, have more, are more and accomplish more than people who don't,

and it doesn't have to be loud or boast. It is a quiet confidence that you are in control of your life and your destiny.

If you have it you know it and if you don't I suggest you get busy and find it.

Tim Connor

GROWING OLDER

The clock ticks and the calendar sheds its months before I even take notice.

The years no longer creep but fly on their way to oblivion.

There are extra grey hairs that laughingly sport their new freedom and a few extra pounds that never were before.

Everyone else looks like they are getting younger as I grow older. The birthdays now come and go without any celebration, just another day to the world but for me a clear signal that time is running out.

I fight the passing of these years in my mind but my body is evidence of their success.

Women who used to be too old to date are now too young. Isn't that a switch.

There is so much more to do with the time remaining.

There is a difference between getting old and growing older.

It is not all in the mind as so many people like to boast. But yes the mind does have a lot to say about which approach becomes our view.

Tim Connor

THE SEARCH FOR LOVE

Everywhere I look, I ask is this the one for me.
I hope and I wonder, I plot and I
scheme. In days past I would try a little harder to make this one
the chosen one.
But I am older now the dust of failed relationships has
settled all around me.
The mist of hopes longed for, yet not realized cloud my eyes.
I am not too old or too scarred to wish for a brief
moment in time, just
maybe this is the one for me now.
All my trying is in vain,
You don't notice my glances, all my dreaming is pain knowing I am
alone and have so much to share and so much love to give.
The nights and days pass
as my love is stored to one day be released. It cries to find a
welcome soul
that will receive my love and repay in kind.
All I ask of life,
is someone to love and someone to share all my hopes
and dreams with,
and yes all my fears and cares. Where are you.
I am waiting.

Tim Connor

BLIND DATES

You called to tell me what you were wearing.
But I really didn't care about the costume that would
mask your realness.

Questions ran though my head. Would you be pretty and nice
and a match for my mind's fantasy.
But the final question, why am I doing this. Blind dates never
have been the high point in my life.

There is always more disappointment than satisfaction and more
unrealized expectations than I ever thought possible.

I see you standing there and I want to turn and run. But I am
stuck, making idle conversation while discussing foolish
superficial topics. Neither of us care, we are filling time.

I am sure you feel as I do that time is moving to slowly.

I'd rather be watching Cheers.

You were everything I knew you would be.
You were not my fantasy but my worst nightmare.

I gave you the gift of my time. You gave me small talk and

an endless array of immature feelings and attitudes.

You did teach me though, in our passing. To never have another
blind date for as long as I live. And for that I thank you.

We part and I finally feel free. Fate brought us together and
separated us again. Your parting words were so
typical of your style and shallowness.

Have a nice life.

Tim Connor

YOU CAN MAKE A DIFFERENCE

Everyone can make a difference.

You can make a difference in the lives of your children by teaching them well.

You can make a difference in the world with all the other voices who echo your dreams and hopes for humanity.

We can all make a difference by holding fast to our values.

But most important you can make a difference in your own life.

By choosing well, listening carefully and acting decisively.

You can make a difference everywhere you look and with everyone you touch.

And making a difference is a role that's easy to fill and worthy of your effort.

Leaving behind lives that are better and richer and that are a witness to the fact that you lived and you loved.

What more is there?

Tim Connor

HERE AND NOW

There is only one place here, and only one time, now.

We all travel in our days to many times and places through the miracle of our thoughts.
Past regrets and future hopes, other loves and cancelled dreams.
Any place other than here is an illusion.
Any other time than now,
is payment on a debt you will never owe.

Past memories push our present focus aside without regard for the beauty and wonder of the moment.
Future plans pull us out of the present reality with the allure that tomorrow will be better.
That we will be better.
That our dreams will become real.

Yet this futile longing and thoughts of yesterday keep our attention
out of the present and away from the joy of our now.

Staying in the present is one of life's important assignments.

Thoughts of mistakes and errors of the past, memories of words that stung and words that were left unspoken wander
in and out of our minds without reason and care.

Oh to be free of the aimlessness of this mental torture.
For once to allow ourselves the happiness of the present reality

one moment at a time.

Tim Connor

THE RITUALS OF LIFE

Showers that soothe my early morning aches and
laundry that waits patiently in the hamper.

Meals to cook and oh so many errands to run.
Dishes to wash and sex that is old and stale.

Conversations that never touch feelings, fears, hopes and
dreams.
All of these and more while I fill my gas tank on the way
to my haircut appointment.

If we were to look at all the time in the pursuit of ritual,
we might just stop one day and scream, enough is enough.

Life is more than routines and waiting in an endless array
of lines.
It could be so much more, but these rituals are never ending,
colliding with the desire for adventure and
a fulfilling life.
Most people lead lives of quiet desperation, chasing
and enduring these necessary yet empty activities.

Why have we lost the
excitement and passion of life.

There are responsibilities and
expectations, there is an endless list of must do's
and should do's. They call to us with their guilt and their sameness.

We must break free of these repetitive
joyless rountines and learn to love our expression through them.

Tim Connor

YOU TAKE A CHANCE

You take a chance when you hope and you take a chance
when you love.
You take a chance when you're alone and you take a chance
when you risk.
You take a chance when you care and you take a chance

when you dream.
You take a chance
when you decide and when you don't.
You take a chance everyday when you go into the world
naked of the costumes that protect your fragile self.

You take a chance when you are a friend and you take
a chance when you commit.
You take a chance when you tell the truth and you take a chance
when you lie.

You take a chance when you are real and self disclose and you take a
chance when you don't.
You take a chance when you fly and
drive and walk across the street. And you take a chance when
you need someone.

Life is filled with risk. Every risk is a chance that must be bourne.
There is no easy way out of this life. And for many
leaving may well be the biggest chance they take.

Tim Connor

BEACHES

I love the sand, so warm and soft upon my feet as I walk the
endless miles in search of peace and calm.

The children play with no cares for time or rules. They grasp the
moment,

as I reflect on bigger questions of life and death, love and loneliness,
and happiness and success.
Their joy is in their time of play as the lines on my face show the
strain of a solitary life.

But I am drawn to these wondrous shores. Is it to find
the child in me once more and the joy of no deadlines,
responsibilities, and fears.

If these children only knew what awaits them on their journey.
Or is it if I only knew what awaits me
at the end of mine.

Tim Connor

THE WORLD MOVES TOO FAST

The world moves too fast.

Planes fly at the speed of sound while no one drives 65 anymore.
The first of the month always arrives before my bank account is
ready.

People rush to marry and then can't wait to leave the bonds
of bliss behind.

The holidays are here while my mind is still on summer

The fashions and the seasons rush to tell their story.
Students are never students but race through time towards
their unknown careers.
Once there, they hurry on to retirement where they
silently wait to die.

Everyone rushes to get where they are going, then rush home
to begin it all again.

We live by the clock and the calendar, clicking off the days
and minutes and years as if we had eternity.

Will the world have its way with us, manipulating our lives
like a feather in the wind.

What's all this rush anyway. All my life I have tried to get
ahead or at least keep up, and all in vain. I'm still behind.

I can't slow the world and its pace, but I can slow me down.
At least I can try.
Time to go, I need to get this poem to the typesetter.

Tim Connor

PLASTIC PEOPLE

There are flight attendants with smiles that fade only as their
shift comes to an end. And politicians who manipulate
words and emotions feeling little of what they say.

There are models who strut and accountants and lawyers
who live in an all too serious world. And there are lonesome travelers
traveling through life with blinders on that protect them from
the need to share.

There are business people who think that what they do matters
and live each decision as a life or death concern.

And let's not forget all the lonely people reluctant to reach out
for a sign of love and acceptance.

Everywhere I look I see plastic faces attached to plastic bodies.
Forced smiles and contrived laughter, suppressed grief and
hidden longing.
Afraid to laugh and fearful of feeling while carefully avoiding
the risks of life.

There are not plastic faces on the children of the world. They
share their joy and pain, grief and sadness, happiness and
fears.
It will take more time for them to learn to be plastic
people. To hide behind walls of insecurity, doubt
and uncertainty.

I want to look behind your plastic face and to know you
but your barrier to authenticity is only broken in the
early morning hours as your reflection from the mirror of life
looks back at this unknown soul.

You may wonder from time to time in this
reflective state, when did this plastic face become you and where
did you lose the real you in this journey called life.

Tim Connor

SINGAPORE

As the taxi winds its way from the airport to downtown
Singapore, I am struck by the endless landscape of
concrete on both sides of the highway. Each of those buildings
filled with hundreds of people and millions of stories.

It goes on for miles as my mind begins to wander. This is my
first visit to this tiny country so far from home. Yet my
host, Vincent, makes me feel instantly at home in his native land.

He has welcomed me with a smile, a warm heart and open arms.
He will be my guide and fellow traveler as I share my wisdom and
self with hundreds of fellow beings searching for answers
to life and success.

The Orchid Hotel will be home away from home for these two
weeks. As we pull through the circular drive he is giving me a
quick rundown on our two-week itinerary. Vincent will soon become
one of my trusted friends.

I love this city so clean and organized. There were Singapore flags
everywhere. Not the country flags but hundred of poles
draped with laundry extending from windows in every
direction. There was lucky square, an entire block of multiple
stories of shops and more shops.

Street vendors, rickshaws, Mercedes Benzes everywhere. And
aromas that would tempt even the most timid visitor, filled
the air.
The evening bazaars and unknown foods bombarded my senses
each day and night. There were new adventures daily
that stretched my imagination to the limit.

The time passed so quickly. On the last day, Vincent who
had selected the restaurants with care each day asked where
I would like to eat my last meal. How about a hamburger and some
french fries. He laughed so we went on to The American Club
for our last special time to share together.

I will miss Singapore with its charm and diversity. I will miss
Vincent and his wife Sally. They were wonderful hosts and
friends.
I hated to leave, but I'll be back soon, with someone
special to share this wonderful country and its people with.

Tim Connor

WHEN I FIRST SAW YOU

When I first saw you, my heart was captured by your beauty.

When we first talked my mind was stunned by your wisdom
as it raced into our unknown future together.

When we first touched, every cell of my body responded
with passion that was new.

When we first made love it was an ecstasy never before experienced.

When we fell in love, my dream of a lifetime came true at last.

Our wedding day was a storybook tale that was the envy
of a disbelieving world.

When you left me, my world was rocked and sent me cascading
through a series of unbelievable emotions that have
scarred my soul and world for all time.

Tim Connor

WHAT HAPPENED

I thought she loved me but I was wrong. She loved who she
wanted me to become
not who I was and who I am destined to one day be.
Now she is gone. I know it is best, but I
still feel the pain.
Is it my ego that is hurt, that she wants someone else the way
she said she wanted me.
Every now and
then,
I see her and my mind is filled with thoughts of what used to be.
She takes over my mind and emotions for a time,
and I find there is both remorse and amazement that what was is
no longer.
How did this happen, or was it meant to be at all.
Looking back,
when I am secure in my thoughts and feelings I know it had
to end, that the passing of two strangers in love could never last.
But I will always wonder, did she only come
into my life to be my teacher. I needed a teacher, but more than that
I wanted a friend and lover.
Now all I have is an enemy, who only recalls the faults and
the mistakes. How quickly
people change and for the simplest and often the strangest reasons.
But it happened, and I move on to better days ahead.
Happier days to come. Her leaving has made room for someone's
coming.

Tim Connor

YOU SAID YOU COULDN'T LIE

I believed you when you said you couldn't lie,

but you taught me that everyone can and does lie when it suits their whim.

You said you couldn't lie,

but you looked me in the eye and denied the truth that we both knew.

You said you couldn't lie,

but your eyes and your absence were a witness to your deceptions.

You said you couldn't lie,

but your words were empty as the evidence mounted against you.

You said you couldn't lie,

but you did to protect your hollow self from being trapped.

You said you couldn't lie,

but you lied.

Tim Connor

THERE'S NOTHING LEFT TO SAY

The days slowly crawl by and the silence is like a midwinter night, cold, still and penetrating my essence like a newly sharpened blade of steel.

Cautiously I break the impasse with words that I hope will reach your heart.
I keep trying to find the words that will touch that part of you that once loved me so passionately.

Your rebuff stills my hopes that you are willing to meet me halfway on the road to our recovery.

I try again to get you to open your mind but your mind is trapped in the desire for a change and your hear me not.

Carefully I find the courage, one more time. I leave my ego and pride behind a veil of hurt and sadness while I test your willingness to forgive.

But your forgiveness is not to be found. It is lost in some distant unknown valley light years from here and now.

The new you I am discovering is foreign to my awareness. How many times must I bury my fear and my desire to salvage our life together.

There's nothing left to say now.

I can't do it all. I need your willingness but you are not willing.

I want your understanding but you are locked in your refusal to try.

There's nothing left to say.

Tim Connor

MR. RIGHT

You are looking for Mister Right.

Sooner or later everyone disappoints and we must go on anyway.
We must love and accept without scorn and support even when it
hurts.

You're looking for Mister Right. Your search will end in frustration.
You will find loneliness in your expectations while you
shape an inner prison of disillusionment for your desires.

You're looking for Mister Right. At first he may seem so.
But with time you will discover, he also will have flaws and
will lead you astray. You see, he will hide them at first or
you will neglect to notice even though he is real.

When you do, if your love is based on your expectations only,
you will again need to look for Mister Right.

You are looking for Mister Right. I wish you luck.

Tim Connor

I SAW YOU TODAY

I saw you today.

I felt sadness, not for me but for your denial of our life that
has past.

I saw you today.

I was struck by your casualness and selfishness for your own
needs and self-centered ways.

I saw you today.

I will never understand how you could close a door on a life
so quickly and easily with no remorse or tears.

I saw you today.

And I said goodbye to all the memories that scarred my heart
and singed my hopes for love.

I saw you today.

I was brought back briefly to your empty loving words of
days gone by. You said you loved me and our time together.
But these were meaningless words that came from a
deceitful heart.

I saw you today.

You are a stranger in my time, an alien in my thoughts and
an intruder in my emotions.

I saw you today for the last time.
I too have closed the door on the pain of our time together
and the emptiness of your love.

Tim Connor

CHARLY

We all need a loving teacher in life who will help guide
our inner search while not letting us live in illusion.

Someone who will listen to our pain and lead us out of the
disillusionments of life.

Someone who will not judge or condemn our faults but
help us see the errors of our thoughts and ways.

Someone who will show us the
light and take our hand as we travel towards it.

I have been blessed
by a wonderful teacher these past months. He has been a friend
and counselor. He has helped me through the tears and
mirrored my weaknesses and need for understanding.

He has been there to watch and support my unfolding and
growth and encourage my realness and vulnerability.

Sharing deep fears and feelings has not been easy for me all these
years. I have kept myself bottled up building pressure with each
new disappointment.

The time was right and the person was you Charly.

I owe you more than I can say. Your caring and honesty
have helped me in so many
ways. Thanks for joining me on my path through life.

You have touched my soul, and because of you
I am learning to know myself better. You have saved me time
and future pain with your spirit and your love.

Tim Connor

SLEEPLESS NIGHTS

The darkness sounds like an alarm waking me from a peaceful
and restful sleep.

I am wide awake,
and for no apparent reason. My mind is like a tornado,
whirling thoughts, people, feelings and ideas in and out of
my head with no concern for my desire to sleep and my
busy day tomorrow.

Frustration builds,
the pillow is not my friend but a foe to be conquered.
Try as I might the battle to force my way back to sleep
is a fruitless struggle.

There must be something
going on in my mind, that my mind chooses to keep hidden.
I search through the random thoughts for a clue to
my restlessness and my turmoil.
My unconscious is working overtime, solving problems,
sending messages to my resentful body and all to no avail.
I only want to sleep.
Finally I let go, and drift back into a state of semi-consciousness,
resting my body as my mind continues its mission of discovery.

What a wonder the human mind. It never rests. It always serves.
It is always ready for the slightest command and biggest
question.

Tim Connor

I LEARNED ABOUT LIFE

I learned about life from my high school football coach.

And I learned about love from my wife.
I learned about sex from my college sweetheart and I learned about pain from my ex-wife.

I learned about stress from the IRS and I learned about success from my mentors in life.

I learned about failure from all my creditors and I learned about joy from my daughter.

I learned about grief from my best friend's death and I learned about compassion from my younger sister.

I learned about lying from my business partner and I learned about work from my dad.

I learned about hope from God and I learned about honesty from every woman in my life.

And from myself I am learning patience, trust and to believe

I've learned a lot but there is still more to learn.

I am a willing student and await my teachers with a open mind and a willing heart.

Tim Connor

TO TOUCH YOU ONCE MORE

The pleasure is intense, the gift of your willingness and the
smoothness of your skin. When we are together,
sharing, touching, I feel free and alive.
The smell and feel of your breath upon my face quiets my fears and
arouses my hopes.
Feeling your soft yet strong fingers entwined in mine, says we are
one.
Our legs together and our feet searching for that gentle touch.

I can't get enough or you. I want to discover every inch
of you slowly yet passionately.

You give me so much pleasure not just for your touch,
but because of who you are and how you love me.

Tim Connor

BROTHERS

Growing up with brothers is both a joy and a challenge.

Now take my younger brother Kevin,
small in stature but a giant in spirit. As I've watched him grow in
maturity and wisdom through the years, I've come to respect him
more than he knows.
He has had his share of pain and success, disappointment and
rewards.

Even though he has
supervised thousands of people and millions of dollars he has never
lost that authenticity that I so admire.

As the years have passed we are not as close as we once were, but
he is only a phone call away in my need and in my success.

Then there's Jack, my older brother, the rock and my mentor.
Although separated by years and distance I always looked
up to him with eyes wide open and a mind ready to learn.

He paved the way,
for me to follow, but I was too wise and too young to know the
value of his lessons.

We've had our differences, my brothers and I, but they have
brought us closer as we all move into the sunset of our lives.

My brothers, I miss them both, our youth together and
our sharing as we pass each other on the highways of life.

When all is said and done, family is what really counts in life.
To be there at all times, in all ways and never judging and always
loving.

I hope you guys like this little poem about you. Although short on
words it is not lacking in love or respect, support and
admiration.

Love you both, hope to see you soon.

Tim Connor

THE WORLD SHARES ITS GIFTS

There are so many gifts that the world shares with us all.

The clear blue sky and a bright orange sunset, a child's smile
and a helping hand from a stranger in life.

Music that stimulates my soul and the adoration of a loving pet.

A dark evening sky filled with the sparkle of a million diamonds
and a warm summer breeze.

The Grand Canyon, Niagara Falls, Pike's Peak and a lonesome
creek that meanders through a wooded paradise.

The open arms of a loving spouse and the support of an unselfish
friend.

There is air to breathe and water to drink and food that tempts my
pallet while nourishing my body.

Everywhere there is abundance. There is plenty for each of us and
no need to hoard.

All we need, to enjoy our share of the world's gifts, is to ask
of life what we desire and open ourselves to each and every gift.

There is no need for envy or jealousy.
The gifts of the world are for everyone but we are caretakers
not the owners of these special gifts.

So enjoy the abundance but care for it, for soon
it will be another generation's turn to have their joy as well.

They will be caretakers as well to feast on these gifts and preserve
them for the next group of caretakers.

Tim Connor

WINTER COMES TOO SOON

The trees are bare, the leaves rest quietly awaiting the first snow.
The nights are longer now and the days brisk with the smell
of the coming winds and sunless skies.
The skies turn grey and my heart is sad.
Here and there a restless squirrel races the clock
and the calendar.
Gone are the peaceful days of summer and fall is now a recent
memory.
I loved the blissful sunshine of the long days and I miss
the color exploding everywhere I looked.

The frost on my windshield is a sure sign that winter covets
its time. There is evidence everywhere that the promised
stillness is anxious for its time.

But winter you have come too soon. I am not ready

for your long nights and bitter days.

Tim Connor

HAVE YOU EVER NOTICED

That lines move slowly when you are behind the clock, and the
higher your expectations of people the greater your frustration
with them.
Time passes slowly when you are bored while you ask where
has the time gone as you indulge your fondest passions.

Have you ever noticed how you block the pain of distant
faded memories that once filled your heart with sadness?

And have you ever noticed that the closer you get to a goal
the more elusive it seems to become?

And when you reach your desires, how their satisfaction is lost
in the search for more.

Have you ever noticed that much of your thinking is just
recycling the same old thoughts that punish your waking hours?

And I'll bet you've noticed that once you solve a problem
another lurks in the wings to take its place.

I'll bet you have also noticed how your life is slipping
past your very own eyes with the speed of light.

But have you taken the time to notice how most people don't really
live but go through the motions living lives of suppressed
desires and subdued anguish for a better life that is always
just out of reach?

Tim Connor

THE LAST LEAF FELL

The last leaf fell today, the final remnant of the passing of the
season.

It struggled to hang on but its time was here.
It was time to let go,
and join earlier travelers who passed before.
As it gently floated through the air to its final winter refuge,
I watched as it surveyed its surroundings and its life. It took
joy in its beauty and uniqueness and repose in its life and
purpose.
As it slowly descends towards a pile of lifeless forms, I noticed
it tried in vain to stall its final reward.
It too now lies lifeless with a conformity that is lost in time.

As it lay there I am also certain that I saw one last gasp
from that solitary leaf. It seemed to say, I have a few regrets.
Next year I'll get it better. I will share more of my
uniqueness and spread more of my love and beauty
with even greater resolve and compassion.

I will love more, be more and live more.

Tim Connor

TODAY WAS A GOOD DAY

My phone rang, a kind hello and a sweet goodbye.
A friendly smile and a familiar nod.
Someone cares, someone remembered.

Today was a good day.

Tim Connor

LET'S TAKE THE TIME

Let's take the time to talk and let's take some time to walk together in the quietness of our love and friendship.

Let's take the time to love ourselves and each other as we meld the union of our spirits.

Let's take the time to pray, thanking God for all our blessings and his care.

Let's take the time to share our realness with each other as we grow in understanding of our needs and desires.

Let's take the time to nurture our world and its fellow travelers as each of us moves into an uncertain future.

Let's take the time to give, of ourselves and our gifts of time, support and encouragement.

Let's take the time to enjoy the gifts of life as we come together in this time and space.

And let's take the time to listen, to our world, its pain and its joy and its hurts and its reaching.

This time is ours and we can use it as we please. So let's use it wisely and let's use it now.

Tim Connor

RAINBOWS

I have seen a few and so have you.
Their colors caress your mind but their miracle is in their origin.

They are a message from God, that there is something good
and beautiful in the rain.
We all have in our life a few rainbows during our times of
trouble.

Next time take a moment and see the beauty, not the pain.
Feel the presence of God not just the coldness of the rain.

And believe, that without the rain, the miracle of the rainbow,
would not be possible.

Tim Connor

MY LITTLE SISTER

She came into the world my mother's prize after 3 boys and 40 years.
She was a joy and a bundle of love and fun.
Her smile brought tears to my eyes as I gazed upon her
porcelain-like body so radiant and glowing.

As I watched her grow into womanhood, I relished her youthful
spirit and generous heart,

Now that she has a family of her own
every once in a while I get to relive those earlier feelings and
memories when I see her children, carbon copies of her mold.

She has been the glue in our family these past years that has held
us all together.

In spite of careers, travel, other families and responsibilities
she has done her best to see that we all never drift
farther apart than the nearest telephone.

But however old she gets, she will always be my little sister,
Marantha.
Loving, supportive, giving and caring.
She has never disappointed me in all these years and she has
always been there when I needed a friendly voice and sympathetic
ear.
Even though she is my little sister, she will
always walk tall in my life.

Tim Connor

MID-LIFE CRISIS

As the 40s speed into the 50s, a change is taking place in the minds
and bodies of many.
The frustration of unrealized goals and dreams adds fuel to the fires
of discontent.

There is a part of us that wants to hold on to our youth, yet our
youth was bathed in emptiness and superficial lies.

There is a part of us that hopes for an endless number of years
to fulfill our fantasies.

Why must this passing be a crisis.
It can be a wonderful adventure of discovery and passion unknown in
our youth.

Just think, you get to take 45 years of experience and wisdom
and use it today as you move into tomorrow.
What a gift,
these years you have accumulated since your birth.

If you are caught in a crisis of the spirit today, just remember

that at least 50,000 people
died in their sleep last night.

Tim Connor

THINGS THAT PUNISH ME

Lonely nights and hotel rooms.
The fear of death and living an unfulfilled life.
Criticism for the sake of criticism.
Dying alone and having to eat mushrooms at a dinner party.
Airplanes that are old and a wife that confronts.

Losing my hair and never seeing my children again.
Uncaring friends and being overdrawn.
Bill collectors that hound and strange new aches.

Extra pounds that are hard to shed
and waking up alone.

Not knowing why you left and where you are.
Unanswered questions and answers that don't work.
Too little time and time to kill.
Memories that fade and desires cut adrift.

Advice from morons and wisdom from fools.
Freedom to choose and too many choices.
An inner voice that counsels while I search for
counsel elsewhere.

Cold days and games people play.
Lines everywhere and an ex-wife who acts like I was never born.

Unreleased passion and hot sheets in summer.
There is more
but I am afraid if I continue I'll get depressed.

Tim Connor

I LOVE MY BOOKS

I love my books. They guide me through the maze of feelings, ideas and thoughts while they push me into my future with confidence and hope.

The stacks sit patiently in my study waiting my attention. Who will be next to occupy my many waking hours of leisure.

They each cry out, me, choose me, I am what you need at this moment in your life. I hold the secrets to your inner struggle for peace and understanding.

As I mentally am drawn to a particular book, I am not quite sure why. Is it the title that knows best what I need for the many questions that bombard my consciousness.

Do books really hold the keys or is it my ego that must search outside myself for the many answers to life's staggering issues.

I don't know, I do know that my books are my friends. They gently teach and support me as I grow through the madness of my life's mission.

My books comfort my pain and my desire for knowing. But, as I read, I often wonder how is this author better aware of my pain and nakedness to the world than I am. And I am the one living this life.
How can they know my needs. We have never met. Could it be that their struggles have paralleled mine, like the endless white lines stretching ahead on a lonely highway toward the final curtain.

They reach out to me with a patient warm embrace. I am not your teacher, but your guide and counselor. You must choose what you will take and what you will leave behind.

All they ask is that I am willing to grow and to stretch my awareness and understanding of thoughts never considered. It seems I have read some of this stuff before at another time by another author. Why must I be persecuted again by this constant nudge from these impersonal pages to reach inside for the answers to my life.
I guess they have the answers after all.

Tim Connor

JIM

One of the real blessings in my life has been the growing
friendship with my friend Jim.

He has always been there with his comforting words, gentle counsel,
loving support and special insight. And unlike other friends
I've had he has opened his wallet in my need.
He has patiently guided me toward a higher path of awareness
and opened my mind to many new ideas and thoughts,
that would one day stretch the very depths of my wisdom.

With all friends,
there are times of discomfort and struggle but he has always
been bigger than our adversity and he serves as a model
for me to follow.

Jim has a kind and nurturing spirit and like all searchers
he shares himself with no demands and no expectations.

My only regret,
is that geography has kept us apart in presence but at least
we have never been far apart in spirit.

Why is that many of the special people in our lives are never
close enough so that we can hug and share our changing lives with them
on a regular basis. To look in their eyes and tell them from
the deepest parts of our hearts that we love them.

Tim Connor

THE SINGLES SCENE

Everyone is looking and few are finding. Everyone is hoping yet disappointment fills their hearts.

Mr. Right is here I know it. If I could only find him in this sea of endless faces. Ms. Perfect hides in the crowd and avoids my glance.

Why am I here. It's always the same. My desire is on fire but my hopes are fading into darkness.

I guess I missed her again. Next week I'll come earlier or maybe later or may be I'll just watch T.V.

Tim Connor

SUMMER HAS GONE AGAIN

The sun moves slowly through the sky warming my spirit and
tanning my body.
I love the summer sun.
I move just a little slower yet deliberately through my days.
I want these sun-filled days to last forever. Yet the sun must move
on to distant lands
to share its warmth with people awaiting its arrival.
I will miss you, your soothing rays and tender nights.

The trees begin their transition sharing their endless rainbow of
color with passersby who
seldom notice their splendor.
The squirrels are busy at work harvesting their bounty for the
long winter ahead. This is a busy time for all.

Nature and creature alike must leave their memories behind.

The long days fade into an early darkness and the nights become
crisp and clear. Fall is on its way.

Frost is just around the corner and it is time to change my
wardrobe.
Summer, I mourn your passing. You came and went so
swiftly. But you will return again and I will patiently await
your coming.

For soon your gentle breezes will once again caress my aging body
and pamper my weary mind.

Tim Connor

SAYING GOODBYE

Goodbye is never easy. Will we meet again as travelers through
    life or is this final picture of you in my mind.
all that I will take with me in our parting.

There is both sadness and joy
in our leaving. Sadness for what could have been and joy
    for what life will share.
I would like to take you with me into the newness of my life.

But it was not meant to be.

Your purpose in my life and mine in yours is complete.
    We must move on. But it is with a heavy heart and a tearful eye
that I will watch as you fade from my view.

Good luck seems so trite. Farewell so insensitive after all we
shared.
A simple goodbye will do.

Tim Connor

TODAY I BOUGHT A PICTURE

The blank wall in my apartment cries out for color and character.
I want the perfect piece to fill that space.

I want a reminder of something to hope for or something lost.

My wall doesn't care.
It knows better. It only wants to bring pleasure.
Today I found the perfect picture. Alive, it stretches
my imagination each time I stop to gaze. Most of the time
however I don't take notice.

Kind of like life in a way. Once we get what we want, we take
less interest daily until one day the picture holds no more
meaning.

Is it time for a new picture or is it time for a new me.

Tim Connor

FRIENDSHIP

If you have a real friend, consider yourself blessed.
True friends,
the ones that share and listen, are rare indeed. A friend can
put you first while they feel your pain and dream with
you as you soar in your fantasy.
They ask nothing,
and they give much. Nothing is too much for a friend.
I've had a few, but
Where are they now.
Were they really ever there.

Some friends are like strangers masquerading as kindered spirits,
taking and never giving. It's ok, I can still be your friend.

A true friend is a gift from God that lasts forever.

Many times just when I think I have one, my hope dies again.
I will be forever grateful for the few I've had along
life's path.

We don't need a stable full of empty friendships, just one that will
share our loneliness and our grief, our burdens and our joy,
and love us for who we are yet encourage us to become all that we can.

It seems so simple,
yet the test of friendship is stern and there are few who
pass the test.

People come and go but true friends last for all time.

Tim Connor

I THINK I THINK TOO MUCH

My mind is a master storyteller. I can take the simplest word or look and create hours of dialogue within me.

Dialogue that often erodes our relationship.

Why is it that most of the stories I create have unhappy endings.

You never know the stories but you are a witness to their control over me.

I would love to have happy endings to all these stories and

all this thinking.

Better still, I wish we were talking.

Tim Connor

LOVE

I want to love someone with every breath I take.
And yes I want to be loved as well.

Where is love to be found. Is it in the arms of my beloved,
or is it knowing that we are both committed to love's long story.

I've been respected, supported, cared about, believed in and
liked.

But as I survey the love's of my life, I now know in my heart
that I have never really truly been loved with a total
uncompromising depth that would give the bonds of true
love time to weave themselves into a tapestry of beauty.

There were always weak strands in the fabric of these loves.
Some so weak that the slightest
tug or stress could snap the bond in an instant. And some
were stronger. They were broken only with the daily
pressures of children and money.
Can love conquer all.
I don't know. A part of me wants to believe that it can.

I would like to have one true love before I leave this
lifetime.
I would like to wake each and every morning knowing that
whatever life brought our way, we would use to
strengthen our love.
I would like to fade into my dreams each night knowing
that my beloved was truly by beloved, my life partner and friend
and lover forever. Those of you who have that,
what a blessing you experience.

As the years pass I have to wonder will I ever have this joy,
and contentment. This security in our mutual decision to love,
cherish and grow together into our independent lives.
Can we be true lovers and not just transitory souls taking what
we can and giving only what we need to before moving on.
Moving on is painful. Even though there is growth in the moving.
I have to believe there is more growth in staying.

Tim Connor

NEW BEGINNINGS

Someone leaves, someone new comes along.

Someone leaves and someone new crosses our path.

Someone leaves and someone new holds us tenderly.

Someone leaves and someone new commits to love.

Someone leaves and someone new leaves.

Life is a series of new beginnings, and oh yes endings.

I hate the endings but I love the new beginnings.

Tim Connor

SANDRA

You came into my life like a sunrise, blessing me with love
and warmth. Your charm and innocence
seduced me into your soul while your passion was irresistible.

We shared so much through the years, life gave us pain and
joy,
frustration and understanding and laughter and oh so many
memories.
We cried and we fought but we always loved.
Life brought us together, who knows why. Then it was over
as quickly as it began.
I was stunned and lost wandering through life without
an explanation, without a purpose.
You were my first real love and you may be
my last.
I thought we would grow old together watching our children
as they made their own way through life.

I have missed so much because of our parting. My regrets are many
but the memories fill my mind,
with sweet joy as I think back on our time together.
Our paths split and we went our separate ways, and then
they crossed again.
Who can say why. You may never know the gratitude I feel
for our coming
together once more.
There is this urge I feel that wants to be with you, but I know
in my heart that the reality of recent events
forbids this outcome.

I loved you, I love you, and I will always love you.
You are a part of my soul, my heart and my life.
I was blessed to share life with you.
And I will forever be thankful.

Tim Connor

I HAVE SPOKEN TOO SOON

Was it my mind or lips that deceived me or my heart speaking
what my mind didn't know.

Too often I have spoken words that stung your hopes.

And I didn't know their truth until later when you
confided in me in our parting,

I am only human prone to err. Have you never spoken out of turn.
Whatever happened to understanding, compassion and love.

Not always for my words but at least for who I am.

Tim Connor

I WISH I KNEW WHY

I wish I knew why people don't understand me. Is it because
I don't really know myself.
My motives are loving and
kind but they are often perceived as selfish and weak.
I give my gifts of sharing, love and understanding but in
return
I am often criticized and overruled.
The days turn into weeks the weeks into years and I am still
the same.
Oh yes, I am different, older, wiser, but still the same.
I want to love, share, a gentle
touch that says you care and a kind word that says you understand.
I wish I knew why I needed this so much. Am I a slave to my
desires and my yearnings. Is there anyone
who can fill this void in me. My head knows that it is up to me,
to fix me
but my heart still hopes that you will be there.
Why is it,
that no one seems to respond to my giving with love, why is it
that it often is so one way.
I used to give my gifts with strings attached. I needed your thanks and
your appreciation.
Now all I want it your loving acknowledgement.
Is that too much to ask.

Tim Connor

THE GHOST OF MY FANTASIES

We all have a fantasy or two. Some reside in the deepest part of our souls while others are light years away from fulfillment.

Yet some may be satisfied in the next room, if we will only ask.

Why don't we ask. Is it because they are safer as fantasies.

When achieved, if they refuse to satisfy, our minds would be deceived, once again.

Tim Connor

The real voyage
of discovery consists not
in seeking new landscapes,
but in having new eyes.

Marcel Proust

ONE MORE STAGE

The room fills gradually at first while I pace the aisles and the
long corridors.
The time will soon be here, it is my turn to once more share
lessons learned and wisdom gained.
There are hopeful faces and people who don't know why they
are here.
I often ask, why am I here as well.
I meet some of the attendees and share superficial words
while my mind focuses on my own reasons for being and being
here. What can I offer these fellow travelers that will
make their journey through life a little easier.

How will I do. Will they be receptive and loving or closed and
critical.
The time for me to begin now closes in like an eagle on its prey.
He will then soar once more to survey the heavens from
his lofty heights.
Will I soar as well. Will my words be right and my emotions
true.
With each new stage, my doubts fight with my confidence.
My self esteem is an open window to these sea of faces.
My vulnerability is on trial once again.
Can I, just once forget me and let God be God in me.
Can my words be his
words or will my ego once again sabotage my realness.
As I manipulate my feelings and massage my words, I pray
that I can reach the hurting souls that have come to grow and
learn, and be.
And that my fears and hopes displayed will be an example for
others to follow.
I will never know.

I am finished now, my time is up. The applause recedes and those
sea of faces leave to continue their lives in some other place.
Did I make a difference this time in just one life.
I wish I could know. It would make all the pain of sharing
and the uncertainty of my fragile message worthwhile.
There will be another stage and a room full of hopeful
hearts. Another chance to get it right.
Why do I think it wasn't right this time.

Tim Connor

IF MY TIME WERE SHORT

I've often wondered if my time were short, how I would feel
and what I would do with the time I had left.

I don't dwell on this time for I know one day it will be
here.
But I can't help thinking from time to time about how
I would spend my last days.

I've had life, and the gifts it has given. Joy, sorrow,
pain and grief, love and laughter.

Life always ends too soon, There is always some unfinished
business, or words left to speak.

Before we have taken charge of all our tomorrows, death
snatches us from the bonds of the earth and our loved ones.

There is not time now for regrets, or going back and no time for
unfinished dreams or unfilled loves. The chase is over.

Then how will I use these precious few remaining days,

To forgive and let go and to get close to God and myself.

To love each moment as a gift from the universe.
And on my last day
I will call everyone I know
to thank them
for their gifts of kindness and sharing themselves with me
and to tell them I love them.

Tim Connor

WHAT IS HAPPINESS

What will it take to find true happiness in my world.
I have longed for love and it has eluded my grasp.

I have searched for wisdom and the questions go unanswered.
I sought fame and I was a stranger in my world.
I thought the answer
was in success, while success left my life empty of the
voices of my loved ones.

I, in my arrogance decided that pleasure and the freedom to choose
my adventures would end my search. But my life refuses
to be a victim of my unknowing ways.

There have been limits on my searching and frustration in the
void that was my becoming.

I have been looking in the wrong places for my happiness.

It is not to be found in the arms of my beloved or the exotic
places I have visited.

It is to be found deep within my being, hidden behind

the curtain of my ego. And until I look inward my unhappiness
will be my constant companion.

Tim Connor

THE MYSTERY OF TIME

What is time but a reflection of my thoughts. It creeps when I am bored and flies when I am with the one I love.

It passes grudgingly as I search for my purpose and it moves with determination once I discover my desire. If there was only a way to reverse this formula.

I want more time, yet I misuse the time I have. I want a clearer vision
yet I cloud my way with doubt.

I can't manage time, it defies my feeble human attempt to harness it.

I can't get more time, God's clock ticks on into eternity.

In reality,
I can't ever use my time up, store it or borrow from the future,
Time is only a notion, a concept or truth.
Then what is left.

I am left with the haunting feeling that I must know myself, and
until I do, my time will not be my friend.

Tim Connor

WHY DO WE WAIT

My daughter cries for my leaving but I am off to work. Her sad eyes follow me as I head into the world of enterprise.
I call back to her, I'll play with you tonight when I return. But her eyes know the truth that I am unwilling to admit.
Later never comes.

My wife called, let's go out to dinner and movie. I have to work Hon, let's do it this weekend. But this weekend eludes us both.

My friend suggests some time together to share and grow together but I have this meeting that I must attend. How's next week.
But next week flies by without a trace.

Why do we wait,
to tell those we love we love them.

Why do we wait to send flowers to funeral homes, when they would have been enjoyed more at an earlier time.

Why do we wait to see the error of our ways until we are too old to change.
Why do we wait to love and accept ourselves, leaving a trail of broken dreams and promises and relationships in our wake.

Why do we wait,
to tell the special people in our lives that they have meant so much.

Is it the rituals of life or just intentions gone haywire that mold our busy but empty lives.
People don't know how you feel until you tell them how you feel.
Why not call someone now or tell someone close how much you care.

Don't wait,
they may not be there tomorrow or you might not be here tomorrow.

You've got everything to gain and nothing to lose. Or you have everything to lose and nothing to gain.

Choose now, but choose well.

Tim Connor

TO BE FREE

In each of us there is an urge to be free. To live life without
worry and stress and distress and pain.

We all want to be free from,

Frustration,
Guilt,
Resentment,
Blame
Fear
Anger
Discouragement
Worry
and freedom from unfulfilled desires.

To be really free
you must unlock the gate that holds your higher self imprisoned
in darkness and anguish.

The key to this gate,
lies deep within your being. It is hidden behind years of
disappointment and unexpressed desires.
To find it you will have to look with courage and calm.

You must persist when you feel that the search is in vain.
For to be truly free the search must begin and once begun you
cannot go back.

And it is not a search for timid souls.

The road inside is cluttered with all sorts of baggage and illusions
as well as erroneous beliefs that have become etched on your
mind.

Your key to freedom lies in your power to control your thoughts.

Tim Connor

WHERE SAND MEETS THE SEA

I have walked the beaches of the world, so pure and white, so relaxing and full of peace.

The view is always the same.

An endless blue horizon that calls to me, be still, all is well.

I will be here for an eternity, and so will you.

Tim Connor

THE PEACEFUL LIFE

Life daily challenges us from without to search, provide, chase
and want.

Success, power, fame and happiness are our goals.
Finding outer peace is like grabbing for the brass ring in darkness
each time you pass.

If peace is not to be found in the outer world it must be reached
in quiet contemplation in our inner world.

The peaceful life,
is a contented life, a fulfilled life, not with desires met but
with wants that satisfy, our urge to be whole and
our need to be free. Free of stress, free of pride and free of ego
and free of the insane need to live our life by other's rules.

The peaceful life is a life of acceptance.
Acceptance of the reality and the realness of life.
Acceptance of the person we are not the person we are
becoming.
It is a life of living here and living now. For there is no other
time and no other place.
There is an easiness in one who lives the life of peace.

An easiness in stride and words, emotions and feelings,
that whispers to the world, no matter what happens in my days and
nights, I live without fear and anxiety, doubt, and
care. I take the world as it comes. It is a life of peaceful
coexistence and passive resistance to all the issues of living.

Tim Connor

ILLUSIONS

What often seems so real is nothing more than an illusion that
betrays your mind and lures your heart.

There are illusions that cause pain and frighten and some that
offer temporary joy that we are living in a real world,
with real people feeling real feelings and expressing real emotions.

Fantasy is illusion, the past with its distant memories is an
illusion and the future filled with hopes and dreams is an illusion.

The only reality is now. The only place
is here. Anything else is like a cloudless sky with no beginning and no
end.

Our reality is nothing more than the projection of our own mind
and its thought energy of stored words and feelings, facts, and
memories out into the world.
Our illusions are not mirrored by others' illusions. They have their
own projections to create from their inner minds as well.

We all think we see, think we hear,
and think we feel.
But there is so
much more that we fail to see, are unable to hear and unwilling to
feel. Life is our personal
interpretation of events, people, sights, and sounds, perceptions
and circumstances
and the value we place on them.

To live a life without illusion you must
know yourself and accept that you will always
be in process as a person. Refining, changing, growing and
developing.

Tim Connor

MY FEELINGS BETRAY ME

Can I ever trust my feelings again.
They have betrayed me so many times.

The fears, the excitement, the longing and the disappointments.

There are too many feelings to list but they all have at one time
or another, led me astray.
Did I create these feelings or did I allow you to create them
within me.
And does it really matter any more.

Tim Connor

WHY CAN'T MEN FEEL

It started long ago when I was just a boy. The rules were
everywhere, be good, be quiet, don't cry and don't express how
you feel. Don't complain and don't be different, don't laugh too loud,
and don't dream too big, you will be disappointed.
Hold you anger and keep your conflict inside.

And don't and don't and don't.
The words ring in my every thought as I struggle to be a man.

If you will please me, I will love and appreciate you,
acknowledge and listen to you.

I had many years to practice my role until my stoic face was like
a certificate on the wall.
My teachers were patient and persistent.

My graduation into manhood was quiet but the world would soon
know I had passed all the tests and was ready to withdraw
at a moment's cue.

I had all the tools,
and was ready to begin.

I had blame, repressed tears and anger,
I had thick skin and the desire to win. I had suppressed
feelings and the competitive spirit. And I had a certain aloofness
that would keep future pain at bay.
I was sensitive and giving but the world was not ready for my gifts.
I was loving and open but they would be long hidden from view.

I was not real, I was not me but it would take years to peel away
the layers of superficial charm and stuffed feelings that
were slowly killing me inside.

I was afraid but unable to admit it. I was angry but unsure how to handle it. I was sensitive but afraid to feel it.
And I had so many feelings but unaware of how to express them.

Yes, I learned all my lessons well. But they serve me not in this new life.
Men don't share with other men, it's not manly, men don't self-disclose, they would rather die young. They don't share their real feelings with women it is a sign of weakness. Men don't share openly with children, we must help them carry the baton
after our passing.

I am tired of being a man locked in this hell of rules and expectations of how to perform and believe. I want to cry, laugh, scream, feel and enjoy life and myself for the first time.

I want to be who I am not who I was programmed to be.

How will I make this 18 inch journey from living my life from my head to living from my heart. It seems like such a short journey and an easy one at that. But there are years of unlived life that need to be set free.
Years of practice at being confident and strong. When I felt weak and insecure. Years of practice being alive when I was really asleep.

I need to wake up. I need to begin again the journey to realhood rather than manhood.

Tim Connor

IT TAKES COURAGE

It takes courage to begin again. But it takes more courage sometimes to carry on.

It takes courage to step into the unknown abyss and schism of life.

In the face of adversity and pain it takes courage to go on one more day. To pick yourself up from the ashes of failure and frustration.

I have felt like quitting so many times. I didn't really want to quit, I just wanted to want to quit.

My faith was shattered and my resolve gone as I faced another day.

It takes courage to be real and to expose your vulnerability to a suspicious universe.

I have felt weak and alone, scared and discouraged.. All that was left was a single thread of hope that I would emerge from this time of stress and pressure in one piece.

I have felt at times betrayed by life, that all my effort and all my time went unnoticed like a shadow in the darkness.

I'll never know, from time to time where I have found the courage, the strength, and the will to go on.

I was besieged by doubt, fear and uncertainty. I even felt abandoned by God.

Thankfully though, He was always there in the middle of my pain and doubt.

I have often questioned, is this failure a sign that it is time for a new direction in life.

Trusting and letting go is so hard sometimes. But to find peace, I must find the courage to stop pushing and know that it even takes courage to be still and listen.

Tim Connor

DOWNHILL SLOPES

I like the winter when it brings the soft powder that carries me
gently down the mountainside.

It covers the once barren slopes that were full of color and
heart.
The air is clear and the chill penetrates my very essence.
The layers of clothing are a poor attempt to shield me from
winter's blast. I am cold but happy.

There is a kaleidoscope of color as I work my way down the winding
hills and smooth manicured highways in the snow.

The colors are ever changing as the other skiers change positions
with a randomness that seems beautiful.

As I glide past the pines, searching for the perfect run, my mind
begins to wander. To other seasons and other times and other
people that have shared this experience with me.

Descending this miracle of God never ceases to amaze me. My
mind is full and yet there is a peacefullness to my thinking.

These brief encounters make the madness of the winter months
almost bearable. I now even look forward to these special
trips to the peaks and valleys.

I even look forward to the shorter days. My aging legs couldn't
take much more without a rest.

This snow covered world is in quiet contemplation, reflecting
on itself and it's mission to please.

I usually take one trip a year to the mountains that pull me
like a magnet to their splendor and their challenge.

This year has been a difficult year, I think I'll take a few

trips to renew my spirit
and refresh my soul.

Tim Connor

There are no maps;
no more creeds or philosophies.
From here on in, the directions come
straight from the Universe.

Akshara Noor

HOMEWARD BOUND

There is something special about coming home. The promise of love
and welcome arms.
And the comfort of familiar surroundings.
Adventure sends my spirit searching but there is a peace
in these walls that I know so well.

My spirit has been stretched by my recent adventure but it
is renewed by my return.

I will rest here until it is time to soar one more time. But each
time I leave, the bonds of home grow more taught and pull me
back sooner than I had planned.

I need both the adventure and the renewal to feel truly free.

Tim Connor

LIVING INSIDE OUT

There are only two ways to live. Either I live from the outside in
or inside out.

The world has taught me to live from the outside in but God
is teaching me to live from the inside out.
You may wonder,
what in the world am I talking about, so let me explain.

When you live from the outside in, every appearance and every
event, every person and every activity is destined to control
your every waking attitude and reaction. You are not the
captain of your ship but a mate taking orders and
direction from a cruel and impersonal world.

When you live from the inside out, you, with all your wisdom and
experience, love and hope, peace and desire are the master
of your destiny.

When you live from the outside in you will always have the luxury
of blame. You can blame the government, the weather, your
spouse and your children, your employer and your neighbor just
to mention a few.

But when you live from the inside out, you alone must take
the responsibility for the quality of your life.

Now you know why so many people take
the outside in option.
But when all is said and done, it really doesn't matter which
you choose because we all must face the reality that we
lived our life, no one else did.
The results come later, how you choose to live and how
you choose to be now will determine your peace, happiness
and contentment.
Ignorance is not bliss,
contrary to popular opinion.
Inside out people don't have fewer problems, less pain or
an easier time. Their life is just as difficult, but getting through their
life is easier.
Learning to live life from the inside out is not easy
but it is worth the effort. And it takes no more effort than finding
and blaming someone else for your struggle and your pain.

Tim Connor

KARMA

They say that we will pay, in another life for our errors and
our mistakes, our deeds done as well as the ones left undone.

This karma, is it real or man's way for explaining the unexplainable.

If I must pay in another life for my transgressions then
why does it matter who I hurt or pain that I cause.
If I must pay, I would rather pay later.

I may not even know the role I play in a future life. I will not be
me but a stranger with my unfinished business.
My errors become his problems and his need for growth.

But if I learn my lessons now I ease his burden. Or do I.
There will be other lessons, higher lessons to learn.

This karma stuff gets real confusing. And who really knows.
No one.
It all sounds so neat to explain my problems and need to grow,
But in reality each of us has his own issues to surmount.

If there is something to all this and I have any say at all.
I would love to go back and find the me I was and give
some advice. Why didn't you learn your lessons well. It is
because of you that I must experience all this stuff now.

Tim Connor

WHEN I AM GONE

Will you remember me when I am gone from this world. And if
you do, how long will it be before my face is a shadow in your
mind and my words like a distant echo in your soul.

Our time is so short and there are so few chances for immortality.

Do not cry for me and my passing. I have left the cares
of this world behind.
And do not regret our
meeting. Our paths crossed and we are both better because of it.

I did the best I could with the time I had. I could have done
more, been more and loved more but my time has come.

I have a few regrets but they can no longer be fixed. The
chance for redoing the past is a wish that will go unfulfilled.

You touched me and I pray I touched you in a way that
when you think of me you will recall with a smile our sharing
and our time together.

As your mind retreats for a brief second, to the experiences we
had together, I hope you will carry my memory

into your life and the lives you touch.

You are my witness
that I lived. Without you, I never was.
My immortality rests with your memory of
me.

Tim Connor

THE SPRINGTIME OF LIFE

The flowers cautiously sniff the springtime air. They have been waiting quietly for their celebration of life. It is their time now, to share their blessings with a restless world.

There is just a hint of green in the patchwork of lawns that dot the streets like a quilt.

The trees urge their blooms to come to life while I pass from the winter to the springtime of my life.

Not a springtime in years, but in spirit.

I see my world with a new vision. A vision of hope and possibilities, anticipation and unfoldment.

It was a long winter. My hopes were smashed into a thousand pieces and scattered across the landscape of all my tomorrows.

But it was a winter of discovery and finding myself and growing through the pain.

There is a newness in this springtime. It is almost as if this is my first chance to smell the flowers and sense the beauty before me.

I welcome this new me in a new world.

It is now time for sowing. For a better harvest this fall I must begin now to take advantage of the spring and all the discovery in the winter past.

I am lucky, I have had many years of harvesting. But this year's harvest will bear much fruit if I will just get started.

Tim Connor

IN TOUCH

I close my eyes as I turn inside while the gentle music soothes my world, a world that is often upside down.

This quiet time of reflection is solace to my spirit and food for my growth.

While I pray and meditate, I am looking for that still small voice within me that will guide and counsel my actions and decisions.

There are times, when the voice is still and there seems to be no connection to the source of my life. And then there are times when my mind tries to coerce the voice into messages that will satisfy my ego's every desire.

I know the answers are there. If I will only be patient and listen in the stillness. I must be patient, for life sends its answers when I am ready.

The answers may come in a person or an idea or a disappointment. They come now or later but they always come.

My role is to fertilize my mind with a receptive clam and wait.

I must get in touch and stay in touch if I am to know the wisdom that my being possesses.

Tim Connor

DEATH COMES TOO SOON

Death you are not my friend. You take and you give nothing back.
Your sting is felt by so many for so long as your newest
victim is yanked from our midst.

What is your criteria for who you take and when.

There seems to be no rhyme or reason to your madness and your scorn.
You take good people in their prime while you leave the
enemies of life to continue their wrath.

You take children, fathers and mothers leaving children alone.
And you take friends before their time.

Don't set your sights on me too soon. I will fight you with
every breath to the end. I have too much left to do, to see
and to learn and then I need to share what I have learned before
I will be ready.
So look elsewhere for now, I will let you know when I am
finished with my life's mission.

Tim Connor

ALL I ASK

My needs are simple and my demands few.
There were times when I thought I needed more,
more of you, more from you and more from life.
As I look over my life,
I find all I really want is,
a smile when I am alone and a touch when I am afraid,
a warm bed in winter and a cool breeze in summer.

Your presence when I am old and a song in my heart.

To know God and understand myself.
A clean bathroom and a soft towel.
Your ear when I am troubled and a hug when I grieve.

A chance to love and the joy of one more sunrise.

To stand for something that counts and to die happy, knowing
that my life mattered.
As my life flashes before me,
and I view the pictures of my past, all I ask is that, I did the
best I could with God's gift of talent, desire and time.

And to know that he is pleased with my humble attempts to learn,
give and love.

Tim Connor

TO DAD

Dad, you've always been one of the most special people in my life.
I've loved you for your strength and I've loved you for your

weakness. I've loved you for your support and I've loved you for
your aloofness.
I've loved you for your helping me see both the best and
the worst in me.

Through the years we've had our differences, but you, more
than anyone,
have helped me achieve any success in life that really counts.

Your example has guided me through the tough decisions
and most of all to bounce back from adversity.

My only regret Dad, is that we didn't show our love to each other
more openly sooner.

As I touch thousands of lives each year from the platform.
for the rest of my life, you will be there with me on every stage
behind every microphone.
And my message will be. Don't wait, as I did for so many years
to tell your Dad,
how much he means to you and to say,
I'm proud to be your son.

I love you Dad

Tim Connor

WHY IS IT THAT

Why is it that couples fight and old people are alone.
And why is it that bad things happen to good people,
while bad people escape.

Why is it that progress brings pain and memories are often
painful.
Why do so many people struggle for everything and some people
seem to have so much, so effortlessly.

Why is it that youth and wisdom pass each other as beacons
in the night, searching some unknown destination.

Why is it that we hurt those closest to us, those that care
and love and support.

And why is it that what we search for remains lost, while what we
need patiently seeks us out.

Why is it so hard to be happy, content and peaceful.
And so easy to feel guilt, fear, resentment and anger.

And why are we afraid of unknowns, when everything we have,
are, and have done were once also unknown.

We must learn to love the questions.

Tim Connor

LONELY IN A CROWD

Glassy eyes surround me everywhere, bouncing from wall to wall
as if there was no one else in sight. But they cautiously
search for a friendly face and an acknowledgement that I am
real and alive.

I am a member in good standing of this elite group. I have
earned the right to stare as well as anyone.
I want to talk and share some news, offer an opinion or change
a view.
I want a chance to leave my lonely ego behind and make a
friend. But no friends here, I've been here before. Only lonely
faces and wandering souls in search of happiness.
We are all caught between two shores, the shores of self
disclosure and authenticity and the shore of some remote
island where we alone reside.
Crowds are a curse to my vulnerability and openness, and a
testimony to my inner struggle.

I must learn to avoid
the crowds, they heighten my need and embrace my desire
for acceptance.
And I'll never satisfy these in a lonely crowd, but within myself.

Tim Connor

A FRIEND RETURNS

We go back many years, too many to track.
We may have been brothers in another life, with unfinished
business to attend.

You were my first mentor, leading and guiding me well.
You helped me travel through the unchartered waters of my
career and life.

You were always there with support and love, encouragement
and an open checkbook.

Somewhere along the way,
we went wrong and the feelings were lost and the contact faded
like an echo dumped into an empty canyon.

Time went by, and I often wondered what became of my friend Bill.
We called him Wish but his given name is William H.

Why did we lose our closeness that once was a sacred
bond.
Then one day you called,
and we began again. Seventeen years had passed, a long time
to be without a friend.

Older and wiser now, the years were both kind and
hard for us both. If we could have been there for each other
we could have shared the glory and calmed the pain.
No looking back, it's only what's ahead that counts.

We are closer now and the bond is no longer corrupt.
We share, counsel, love and support. Knowing when to listen
and knowing when to talk.
My friend is back. I missed you Bill.

Your insight, your courage, and your honesty are welcome
friends as well.

Life sure is funny sometimes. Moving people in and out of our
life with some chaotic ritual that no one understands.
I'm just glad you're back.

Tim Connor

I'VE GIVEN TILL IT HURTS

I've stopped counting all the ways and all the times I have
shared, given and supported. Friends and strangers alike
have been the beneficiary of my gifts. Gifts of love, time, caring,
and cash.

Through the years I have given more than I have received.

In the early years, I'll admit that there were strings on my
giving and expectations, that you could never know.

But as the years have passed, I have seen the error of my selfish
ways and grew tired of the unfulfilled promise of your return.

Now my gifts are from the heart. I have left my ego behind,
like so many other childish games.
But the disappointments still surround me.

Why can't you be like me. A note, a call or even just a
friendly thank you. It takes so little to acknowledge my gifts.
Am I doomed to give and seldom know the joy and pleasure
of your appreciation.

It hurts
to give so much so often to so many and receive so little.

In life there are givers and there are takers.
The givers give and the takers take.
I am a giver, always have been and always will be.

So I must learn to accept this curse and the pain of this
lifetime ritual.

But acceptance will never erase the pain,
only shroud it in the blackness of the night.

Tim Connor

ANOTHER MOUNTAIN TO CLIMB

I love the feeling of exhilaration when I finally reach the top
of another majestic peak. Whether on skis or on foot the
feeling and the view is always the same. What wonder.
The world looks like it is standing still from this distance.

So pure and bright. Though the climb is slow and marred with
potential disaster the top is worth the trip. The color, the
vastness and the splendor fill my eyes and heart.
I want to stay and feel the heavens and talk with
God.

But in the distance I see another peak that beckons to my soul.
There are more mountains to reach and struggles to endure.
I cannot rest too long here upon this last achievement.

Must I climb another mountain. I can never climb them all.
Soon I must rest in the bosom of life who cradles me with
loving arms.

I'm tired of climbing now. I have paid my dues and proven
I am equal to the task,

It is time for wisdom not brawn, patience not rushing and love
not selfishness.

I will never forget the thrill of the climb and the view from the crest
But I am finally free of the need to climb and prove my worth.

It is your turn now.

Tim Connor

THOSE OLD SONGS

Somewhere in a corner of my mind the old songs and their words
have a special meaning.
They remind me of happy times and a first date and sad times and
of your leaving.

The song writers must know me well, for their music
can make me laugh and bring tears, tug my heartstrings
while I get lost in their melodies.
I wonder what will today's songs as memories bring.

But the old songs will endure for they recapture for an instant
my life when love was new and hopes were smashed.

They are enshrined, these old songs, like a treasure
in the corner of my mind. The only key to memories released are the
poignant words written by some stranger to my life.

Tim Connor

THE SIMPLE THINGS

Life is so beautiful, it shows its splendor
in so many simple ways and with so many simple things.
The sunset I
watch with awe, the laughter of a child. The ripples
on the water from a lonely duck wash sleepily against
the shore.
My daughter called today to say hello and the
waitress seemed glad to see me. A
friendly chat with my neighbor.
We are all on the same path together. Some of us see the
simple beauty and some of us miss it because of the chase.
It's the journey that counts, yet I have missed so many of the
simple things along the path.
The smile I missed,
the word not spoken, the hug withheld, the one I
longed for. The joy that can never be, because
I missed the simple opportunity to see.
Regrets, I have a few, did I cheat myself
by thinking that the simple things would always
be there.
They are now like a fading distant fog masking their
image and hiding their sweet memory.
Today will be different. I will
inhale each moment and its beauty as if it were
my last.
Today
I will notice the simple things, for in an instant they will
be gone again.
I will notice and capture the simple things in my world
before it is too late.

Tim Connor

ARE MY DREAMS DYING

So many dreams so little time left. Choices must be made,
the time is drawing near.
But my mind refuses to settle for less.
Deep within me rests the hope that my dreams are alive and well.
The calendar screams, no, time is running out. Act now,

or the ghosts of your dreams will haunt your eternity.
Age has nothing to do with my dreams. It is only a

convenient way of keeping score. I must surrender to the calendar.
It is winning.

Tim Connor

THE FEARFUL LOVER

Cautiously I try again, to test the unchartered waters
of a new relationship. The memories of past mistakes and
the pain of broken promises haunt my vision and my need to
be loved and accepted.
These fears could be transformed into confidence with a
simple smile and a welcome nod.

How can you know
my needs and my desires. I am not even sure lately that
they are real, but ghosts of past frustration and fantasies
left unsatisfied.
Slowly I step into my future with you, aware that your
past brings similar hurts and wants that I must recognize
and accept.
Our paths have crossed. We share a common time and space
in this vast universe of possibilities. It has brought us together,
to share and grow.

Let's slowly come together like a gentle summer breeze.
No expectations and no pressure, no agendas and no fears.

We are new, we have never been, let's leave the history of past
loves and disappointments where they belong, In the
desert, to die a quiet death.

Tim Connor

TO MOM

As I look back over the many years of my life that we have shared,
I can't help but remember not just what you did for me but
how what you did is helping me become a better person each day.

I remember your sacrifice, putting everyone else first, even
when you deserved more for yourself.

I remember your pain, the pain of watching me struggle through
life's journey. Wanting to help me, but my youth and arrogance
got in your way.

I remember your support, even when you knew I might be wrong.
You never doubted my goals or my ability. You were always
there.

I remember your feelings,
feelings of happiness on my success,
feelings of frustration on my failures.
Feelings or hope for my future. And feelings of love because that
is what you do best.

I remember your love, But most of all I remember your love of me
not just for my achievements but for my struggle.
Not just for my success or because I hit bottom and needed
your love,
but because you are one of God's special children, you are my Mom.

Mom, as I look ahead, I want you to remember,

your love, time effort and support was not in vain. As I travel
life's highway each day, I realize how special you are to me.

Thanks Mom for a job well done.

I love you Mom.

Tim Connor

I FELT SAD TODAY

I sat with anticipation waiting for you to appear.
Our newness still fresh in my heart.
But you were not the same. Your greeting was cool and your
eyes looked past my glance as if surveying some distant shore.
You avoided my touch as if we were strangers.

My mind raced with questions as we sat side by side.
Was it something I said or did at our last meeting that
has caused this distance,
and turned your passion into a faded memory.
I had so much hope for us that we would share so much
together. Was that a dream that must disappear with the stars.

I wanted to talk but your mind was busy somewhere else.
You seemed rushed. So I waited for a clue. It didn't come.

We parted with a formal goodbye, as my heart seemed to break
one more time. How much more can my heart take before
it shatters into a million pieces like an evening sky full
of distant diamonds.

You said you'd call,
but something tells me the spark that was beginning to glow
into a fire that would light my life is now as cold as the
winter snow.

My sadness today, for what could have been, fills me with
a heaviness that I have known all too well
in times past.

Tim Connor

You cannot transcend
what you do not know. To go beyond
yourself, you must know yourself.

Sri Nisargadatta Maharaj

ST. PATRICK'S MISSION

God made the heavens, the land and the seas and lovingly
Ireland, too.
A garden spot in a troubled world with its hills and its dales
and its morning dew.

To guard, to protect and preserve it He sent Patrick and said
with a smile, "I am sending you on a mission of love to a place
called Erins Isle. Watch over the hills and the people too, work
with love, devotion and care to make sure it's a land
of smiles and laughter."

Now St. Patrick did as directed, with this we can all agree
for Ireland still prospers despite years of struggle, strife
and pain.

Some day when the world is free, so will this tiny isle be free
of conflict and unrest.

It will share its bounty and spirit with untold
guests.
Who will leave refreshed
and touched by its charm.

Tim Connor

CONCLUSION

We have come to the end of our journey together. But your journey into the rest of your life is just beginning. I don't know what you felt, thought or learned as we have walked together through these pages.

It is my prayer for you that whatever you experienced that had a positive impact on you, you will carry these new feelings, insights and attitudes with you as you continue to walk easy through the rest of your life.

We are all here on this earth for a very short time. I believe our mission and purpose is to learn how to live life from the inside out and not the outside in. To learn to give and receive love and to learn and share what we learn with our fellow travelers.

Even though I don't know you I have shared my deepest dreams and fears with you because I believe we are all connected in some way in this vast universe of space, time and thought.

In many ways I am you and you are me. We have had common experiences and we all breathe the same air and look at the same stars each night. We may never meet in person but you have given me the privilege of meeting you through these poems. And for that I will be forever grateful. Some people come into our lives to teach us and others come into our life for us to teach them. I was not the teacher in our relationship but the student.

May God bless the rest of your walk through life.

Anything can
be achieved in small,
deliberate steps. But there are
times you need the courage to take
a great leap; you can't cross a
chasm in two small jumps.

David Lloyd George

TRAINING ASSOC. INT'L INC PO BOX 1425, ANN ARBOR, MI 48106
313-930-0880 • 800-222-9070 • 313-930-1863 (FAX)

TITLES BY TIM CONNOR, CSP

BOOKS AND MANUALS	PRICE	QTY.	AMT.
When the Student is Ready the Teacher Appears Volume I	$ 15.	______	______
When the Student is Ready the Teacher Appears Volume II	15.	______	______
Walk Easy With Me Through Life	15.	______	______
The Voyage	15.	______	______
The Soft Sell	20.	______	______
Personal Growth Manual	10.	______	______
Selling With Style and Substance	6.	______	______
A Short Course on Effective Management	6.	______	______
AUDIO AND VIDEO CASSETTES			
Search, 8 Cassettes	85.	______	______
The Soft Sell Sales Course, 12 Cassettes	195.	______	______
Sales Development Skills, 6 Cassettes	70.	______	______
Personal Development Skills, 6 Cassettes	70.	______	______
Management Development Skills, 6 Cassettes	70.	______	______
Tim Connor Live, 4 Cassette Sampler	45.	______	______
Becoming or Achieving, Video	49.	______	______

10% Discount For Orders Over $100.

SUBTOTAL: $ ______
LESS DISCOUNT:
ADD SHIPPING: 5.00

TOTAL: ______

TO ORDER

Name ______________________ Tel ______________

Co ______________________ Position ______________

Address ______________ City/State/Zip ______________

PAYMENT METHOD

❒ Enclosed is my check for $ ______________

❒ Charge My: VISA MC AMEX (CIRCLE) No ______________

Signature ______________________ Ex. Date ______

❒ Please send information on Tim's Speaking and Training Presentations.